A Brief History of Protest Art

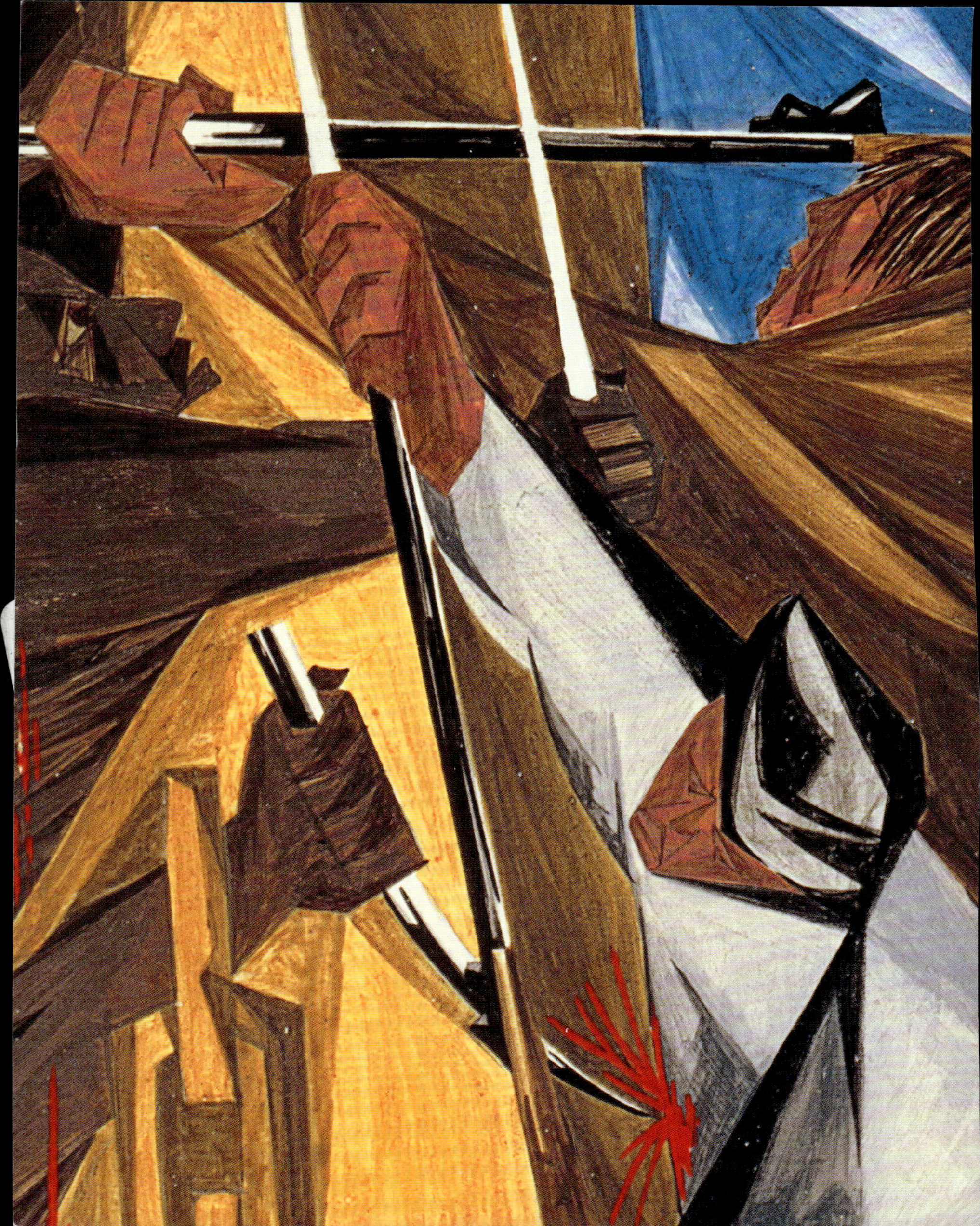

A Brief History of Protest Art

Aindrea Emelife

First published 2022 by order of the Tate Trustees
by Tate Publishing, a division of
Tate Enterprises Ltd, Millbank, London SW1P 4RG
www.tate.org.uk/publishing

A catalogue record for this book is available
from the British Library

ISBN 978 1 84976 782 8

Distributed in the United States and Canada
by ABRAMS, New York

Library of Congress Control Number applied for

Senior Editor: Emma Poulter
Production: Roanne Marner
Picture Researcher: Deborah Metherell
Designed by Johanne Lian Olsen
Colour reprographics by Altaimage, London
Printed and bound in Italy by Printer Trento S.r.l.

Front cover: Peter Kennard *Protest and Survive* 1980.
See p.68
Back cover: Dustin Klein and Alex Criqui *Reclaiming the
Monument* 2020. See p.150
Frontispiece: Jacob Lawrence *Struggle: From the History
of the American People* 1954–6 (detail). See p.30

Measurements of artworks are given in centimetres,
height before width and depth

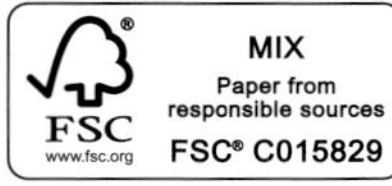

Contents

My Labour Is My Protest

Works

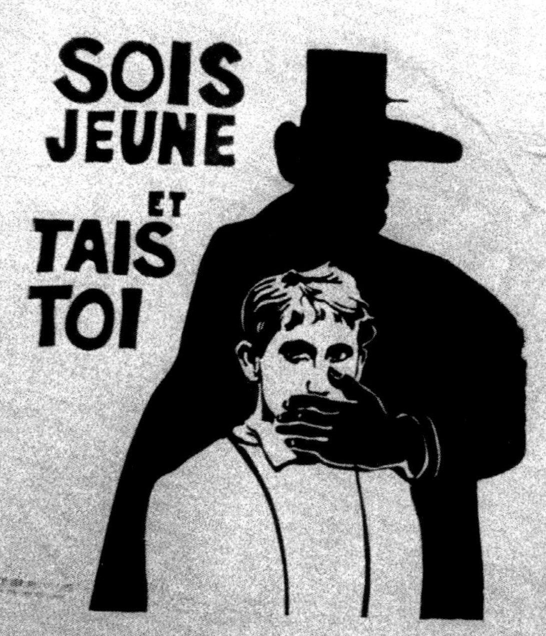
CE N'EST QU'UN DÉBUT
LE COMBAT CONTINUE
SOIS JEUNE ET TAIS TOI
pouvoir au peuple PSU
ACTION
"Il n'est pas de sauveur suprême,
ni dieu, ni césar, ni tribun.
LUTTE
L'ELA

My Labour Is My Protest

Revolution posters which lined the streets in Paris during the general strikes in May 1968 (see also pp.16–18)

We are living in the age of protest. Though, in truth, humans have sought to protest about the status quo throughout history. Indeed, the urge to change the world is at the core of what it means to be human. From the very first marks we made, with cave paintings, humans have recognised the ability to communicate through art, subsequently spurring the realisation that we, as humans, can change the world; and that *we* matter, and *we* matter together. This is central to the idea of social and community change.

It seems unquestionable to consider that art can be made and not be political in some sense, especially when we are living in times like these. Recently, around the globe, radical and revolutionary movements and uprisings, urging actions from police reform to climate change to racial equality with the Black Lives Matter movement, have commanded a place in the mainstream. The call to arms by these important causes can no longer be ignored; especially in the wake of a global health pandemic that shifted our perspectives as we sought to ask ourselves: what really matters?

For too long, the world has sought to be apolitical. We have distanced ourselves from politics and moved towards apathy. We think of weapons, violence, warfare and disease as terrible dangers, and indeed they are, but we can take measures, within reason, to avoid them. But once apathy takes hold of us, we must be wary. Apathy presents real danger. Apolitical, apathetic... we must distance ourselves from being a-anything.

But to the artist, there should be no danger of apathy. Through art, the artist has been given the freedom to communicate and disseminate powerful messages. For art and protest are forms of political thought. They are both potent and make apparent the deep inequities, injustices and truths of our time. The title of this essay is 'My Labour Is My Protest', after Theaster Gates's exhibition of the same title, at the White Cube in London in 2012. Gates's work in this landmark exhibition – which included *Raising Goliath*, a work that utilised theatrical pulleys to suspend a classic red fire-truck from the gallery's ceiling and, in beautiful contrast and harmony, a huge metal container which housed hundreds of leather-bound issues of African American magazines, such as *Jet* and *Ebony* – revealed that if art can change us, it is the labour of the artist that has the power to encourage and effect this change. The archive presented encapsulated some key issues of Black identity and became a poignant reminder that the subjectivity of history makes it too easy to forget the many corners of the human experience. Remembering is protest; listening and learning is progress. The show's eponymous work, *My Labor Is My Protest*, saw Gates source and park a yellow fire-truck in front of the gallery and partially cover it with tar, a material associated with slavery. The work was particularly poignant since the fire-truck was decommissioned from Birmingham, Alabama, following the nightmare that ensued in spring 1963 when the peaceful demonstrations of civil rights activists were met with a violent response from the police, who used fire hoses and police dogs to disperse the protestors. At the core of these powerful works is the idea that social change can come about through artwork: Gates's labour is his protest.

Why then, is it the duty undertaken by the artist to catalyse change? Perhaps because art has the enormous potential to shift society. It can put us in a chokehold, challenge and rearrange our thoughts and beliefs, complicate our understandings of the world and leave us changed and inspired, wondering and questioning.

Defining Protest Art

Art has been used increasingly by political movements to circulate ideas, messages and beliefs. I consider *The Death of Marat* (p.10), painted by Jacques-Louis David in 1793, to be one of the first purely political paintings. David, the official artist of the French Revolution, painted the death of Marat, his slain friend, with clear political intent – as tribute and as revolutionary propaganda. The neoclassical painting was created in the wake of Marat's assassination, casting the revolutionary as a flawless martyr whose political activism is memorialised. It remains both one of the defining images of the time and a pinnacle of protest painting in its early stages.

To many artists, art is a sign of resistance to a hierarchical, global standardised political model. Art is most raw and potent when it acts as a secret agent, luring us in with beauty or some other pretence, and then intervening with our inner-held conventions, some of which are undoubtedly, and unbeknownst to us, intertwined with histories of dominance and subordination, and inclusion and exclusion. In this artistic intervention, the artist destabilises and challenges the status quo.

Immanuel Kant, the great Enlightenment philosopher, describes art as unable to be pinned down, and it is exactly this that makes art political and gives way to the idea that art can be a form of protest. The political was thought of as a space for clear argument, and so could be separated from the messiness and uncontrollable nature of art. In contemporary thinking, the fact that art is disorientating and confusing and messes with our head a bit is not only what makes it appealing, but what makes it

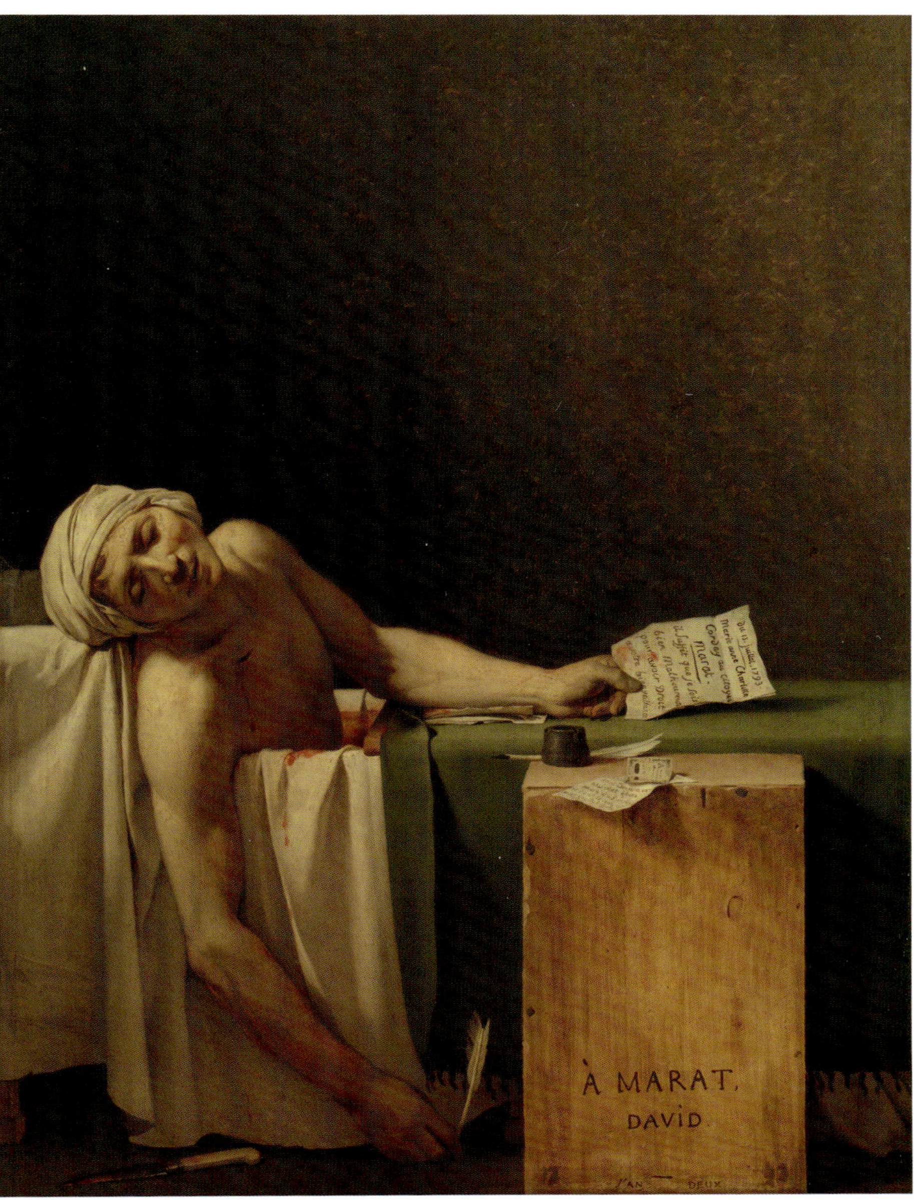
Du 13 juillet 1793
Marie Anne Charlotte
Corday au citoyen
Marat.
Il suffit que je sois
bien malheureuse
pour avoir droit
à votre bienveillance.
À MARAT,
DAVID.
L'AN DEUX

politically powerful. If the struggle against political power and structure is seen as Sisyphean – an impenetrable, rolling force that seems evermore futile each time the rock reaches our/Sisyphus's feet – then protest art is the shining beacon of hope to keep us going. It's just the thing to destabilise. There is a call to be heard and seen at the core of many artworks.

When considering 'protest art' and the historical resonances of that term, and the possibilities of this form of art, one cannot help but think of Pablo Picasso's *Guernica* 1937, one of the most recognisable iterations of which is explored in this book (p.24). Picasso's momentous, chaotic greyscale painting was an artistic revolt against the bombing of the Basque town of Guernica during the Spanish Civil War (1936–9). Unapologetically personal, and thus political, the frieze has become intertwined with the Spanish Civil War protests, and even toured to engage audiences and raise funds for the Spanish war relief. It is the epitome of 'protest in paint' and has a lasting legacy as an icon of revolt. In 1970, at the Museum of Modern Art in New York, the Art Workers' Coalition decided to stage a protest in front of *Guernica*. The protest was in response to the Vietnam War, their belief that the museum was complicit and also the image culture surrounding the war. The group stood in front of the painting and handed out a now-canonical poster known as *And Babies*. The iconic anti-Vietnam War poster consisted of a photograph taken by an army photographer in Vietnam of the My Lai massacre, which was overlaid with quotes from an interview about the massacre. It uncovered and confronted the senseless killings of innocent people, revealing a darker side of humanity. In light of this, can we consider actual protest activity as art?

Protest is not the same as political engagement by an artist; many or most artists are politically engaged. Joseph Beuys (1921–86) is a great example. He gave lectures and made art about ecology prior to co-founding the Green Party. The legacy of the Green Party lives on today, and can be considered his most enduring work. These acts themselves are not protest art as characterised in this book, but they are great examples of a holistic dedication by the

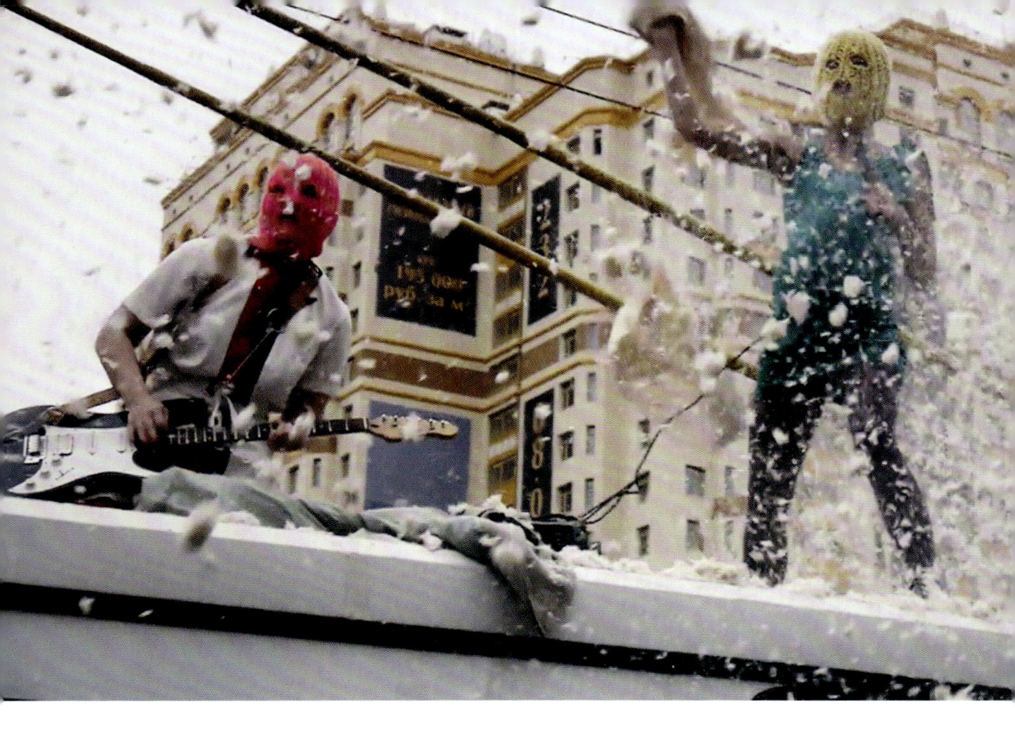

Pussy Riot
performing
on a trolleybus
roof in Moscow
2011, from
*Pussy versus
Putin* 2013
63 min
Gogol's Wives
Productions

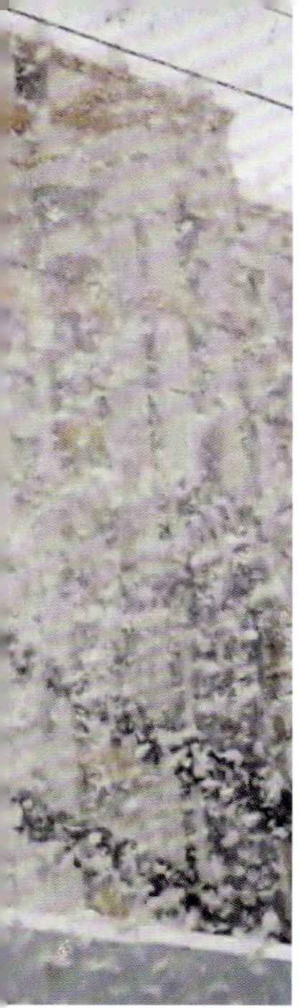

artist to expand the art practice to a social practice and challenge what art can be. For the purpose of this book, I have not considered such endeavours as protest artworks. Though, I would conjecture that we should look to expand what we consider as an artwork, as the definition and characterisation of this term has evolved and changed drastically throughout history, and continues to do so.

Creating art is a civic act – at its conception, production and execution. Protest is fluid, forceful, snappy and provocative. It is ever present, and recurrent, and appears when the social contract has been violated. It disrupts the structure that seeks to control. It is a revolt; a rupture that emerges when society is demanding that something needs fixing.

There is power in numbers – collectives, such as feminist art group Pussy Riot, who bravely sought to punk the system during what was widely perceived as an authoritarian turn in Russian politics from 2012 to 2015. Gaining international fame as activists and calling attention to various political causes, the group were perhaps best known for their usurpation of the Cathedral of Christ the Saviour, where they protested against the increasingly close ties between the Church and the state. The colourful group of five, dressed in brightly coloured balaclavas, baggy dresses and tights, jumped the gate and headed straight for the sacred altar, an area from which women have been traditionally barred, to sing and dance in wild abandon to their song 'Punk Prayer: Mother of God, Drive Putin Away'. Notably, just three weeks before the presidential elections were due to be held, they made their voting sympathies clear. Interestingly, the performance itself drew less attention than their indictment and imprisonment, which the media paid close attention to, but they did garner the support of high-profile artists, governments and celebrities, as global protests for solidarity took place on the streets of New York, Canada and Scotland, awash with balaclava-sporting fans and advocates. Putin, ultimately, won a third term in power, but Pussy Riot, after a two-year imprisonment for two of its members and charges for the other three, still seek to rock the system. Protest can encourage change; but despite

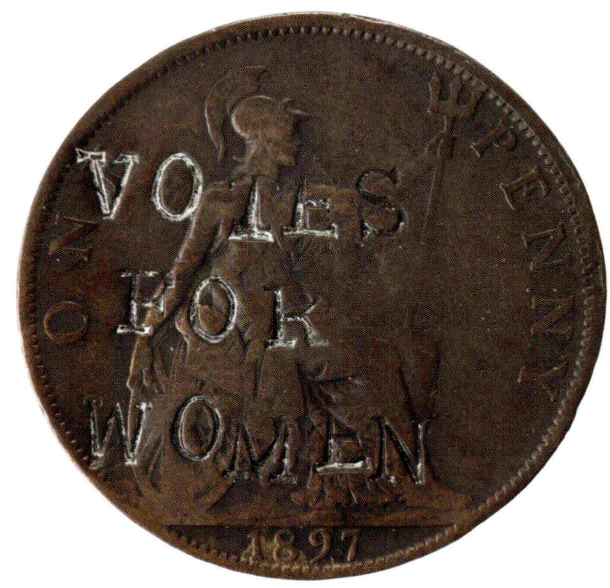

Left:
Victorian copper
penny (1897)
stamped with the
phrase 'Votes
for Women'
c.1913–14

Right:
Jenny Holzer
b.1950
[No title]
1979–82, from
*Inflammatory
Essays* 1979–82
Lithograph
on paper
43.1 × 43.1

the wide-ranging political values of people, the need to speak out and be heard is at the core of the human experience. There is an element of activist in all of us.

Indeed, some of the best protest art was done by activists we may never know the names of. In 1903, you may have been handling coins in your purse, and on closer inspection of one of the coins, you might have discovered the invocation, the demand for a right, 'VOTES FOR WOMEN' engraved on the shiny surface (above). These coins, perfectly ordinary pennies from the Mint, were civil disobediences (defacing a coin was a serious criminal offence) that discreetly impacted when you might least expect, circulating the message of the campaigners via small change. The purposeful decision to stamp on small change rather than silver coins is notable: it meant the message was less likely to be taken out of circulation by the banks, ensuring it circulated for

IT ALL HAS TO BURN, IT'S GOING
TO BLAZE. IT IS FILTHY AND
CAN'T BE SAVED. A COUPLE OF
GOOD THINGS WILL BURN WITH
THE REST BUT IT'S O. K.,
EVERY PIECE IS PART OF THE
UGLY WHOLE. EVERYTHING
CONSPIRES TO KEEP YOU HUNGRY
AND AFRAID FOR YOUR BABIES.
DON'T WAIT ANY LONGER. WAITING
IS WEAKNESS, WEAKNESS IS
SLAVERY. BURN DOWN THE SYSTEM
THAT HAS NO PLACE FOR YOU,
RISE TRIUMPHANT FROM THE ASHES.
FIRE PURIFIES AND RELEASES
ENERGY. FIRE GIVES HEAT AND
LIGHT. LET FIRE BE THE
CELEBRATION OF YOUR DELIVERANCE.
LET LIGHTNING STRIKE, LET THE
FLAMES DEVOUR THE ENEMY!

many years, perhaps even until the law that granted women equal voting rights was eventually passed, as late as 1928, and beyond, memoralising this protest.

Stealthy protest is also present in the work of the Guerrilla Girls (p.80) and Cildo Meireles (p.50), the surreptitious subliminality of which is especially powerful: it hits you when you least expect it.

And so, to define protest art, we can consider the parameters of an artwork that uses canonical or identifiable artistic forms to protest against or disrupt politics, or educate and/or encourage the viewer to look at the world in a different way. This is probably why so much of protest art includes words; it is the familiar language of protest whether printed or disrupted via projections (Jenny Holzer, pp.15 and 110), employing the visual language of marketing (Barbara Kruger, p.84) or punched into coins in the name of suffrage. Words are captivating and instantly arresting as our eyes naturally seek to decode and decipher texts. To disrupt the traditional modes of reading, and make it look different, is to grab and keep attention.

Protest art complicates rather than simplifies. It should usher us forward to the unseen and the unknown, or it should address the known, and urge us to question this reality, so alternative understandings of the world and the way we live may occur. In shaking up our reality and reinterpreting the world anew, the artist reveals existing power relations within society, determining what is worthy of recalibrating. What would it be like to see a decommissioned fire-truck from the Birmingham Alabama Riots, right before your very eyes? Would it bring the harrowing story to life? Can you hear the screams of protestors, exercising their right yet blasted with the potent power of the fire hoses? How does it feel to confront this reality? You can read an article, but how does the physical presence of these items affect you? When they are right in front of you, can you deny, can you feign ignorance, can you look away? Gates activates these responses in his work (pp.116–19), but so does Jacques Louis-David in his depiction of Marat (p.10), as well as Leon Golub, in his arresting images of police brutality (p.76), and Philip Guston in his forceful recognition of the nonsensicality

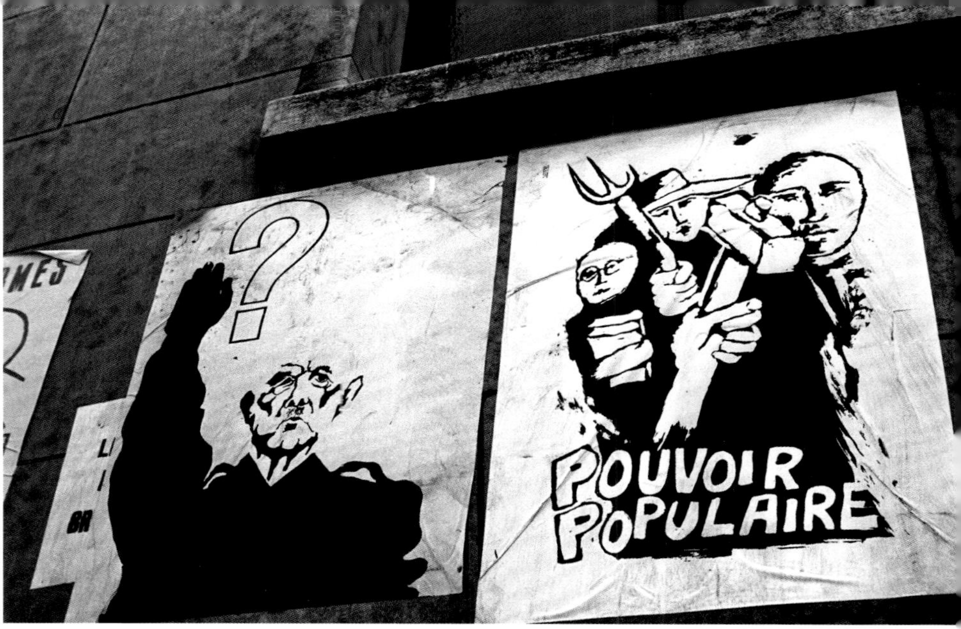

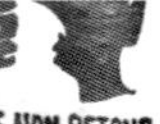
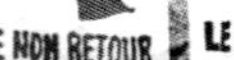

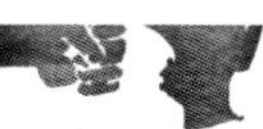
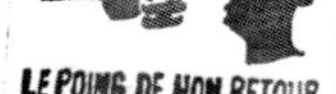
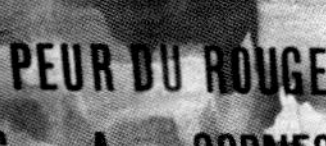
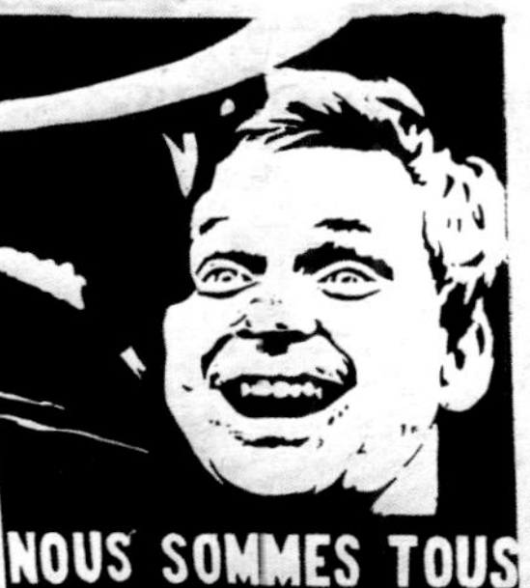

?
NOUS SOMMES TOUS
"INDÉSIRABLES"

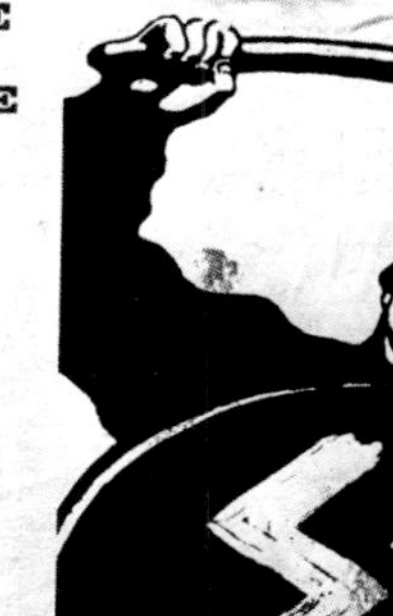

POUVOIR
POPULAIRE

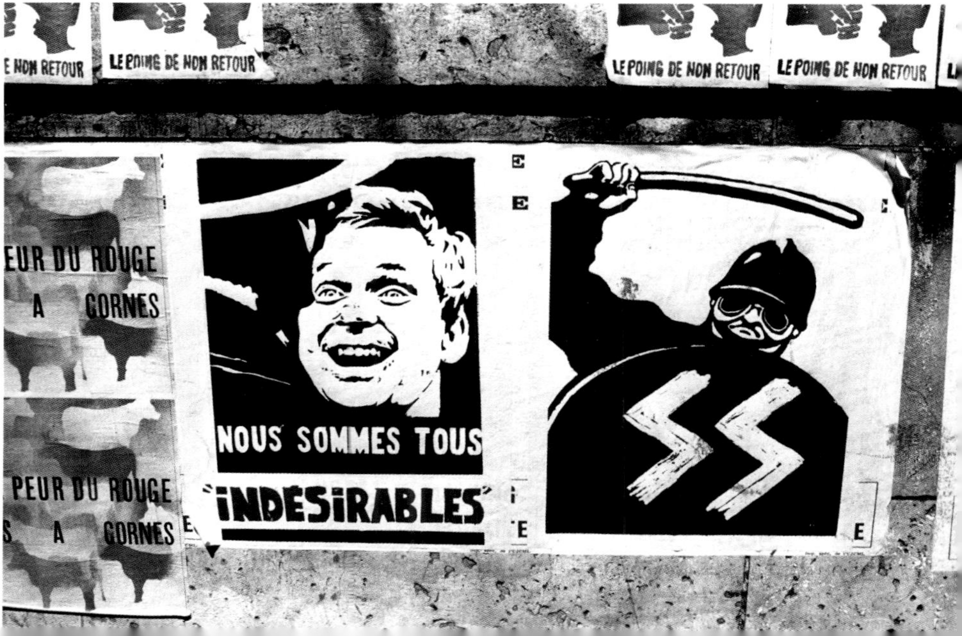

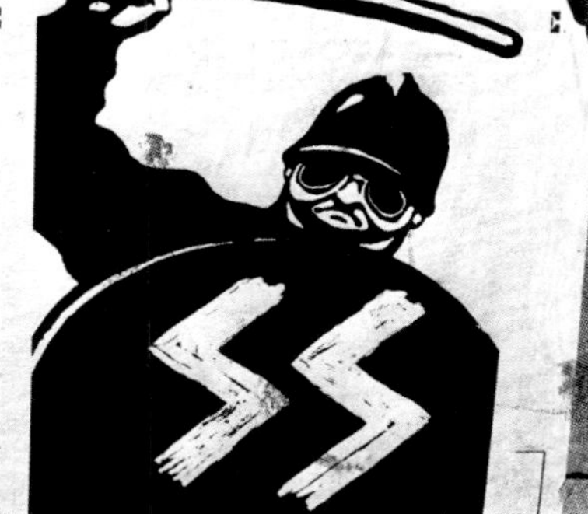

LE POING DE NON RETOUR
LE POING DE NON RETOUR
LE POING DE NON RETOUR
E NON RETOUR
EUR DU ROUGE
A GORNES
PEUR DU ROUGE
S A GORNES

of racism, and the hateful, terrorist conduct of the Ku Klux Klan (p.46). Through their art, these artists protest against injustices and inequalities, raising questions for the viewer in many varied ways. There is a critical ingredient to protest art or a moralising intention. Simply, the art or the artist must seek to catalyse political change.

One of the most democratic forms of protest art is the poster. In May 1968, a group of students from L'École des Beaux-Arts in Paris, France held a series of student strikes in retaliation to clashes with university administrators and police. The government, under General de Gaulle, attempted to stop the student strikes through forceful police intervention, but this exacerbated the situation, and the grievances evolved, becoming ever more political, and kick-starting a revolution. A general strike by the students was held on 13 May, French workers followed shortly after, and this resulted in eleven million workers striking for two weeks, leaving the government close to collapse and fearing a civil war. General worker strikes had already caused disruption, as the working classes pushed against a political move to conservatism and authoritarianism. The later strikes, in tandem with the student protests, culminated in one of the largest general strikes and the first wildcat strike in French history. The posters that covered the streets of Paris during this period became the defining imagery of the time, and greatly influenced the protest imagery that has followed since. Refreshed night after night, a self-named group, the Atelier Populaire, took over a Parisian lithography studio and designed and printed thousands of posters to wallpaper Paris with their call to arms. The designs harnessed simplicity to focus on the message, usually adopting the format of a single-colour screenprint with block text – refreshingly crude, quick to make, even quicker to circulate (pp.6 and 17). The posters represent the urgency and energy of the apotheosis of this counter-culture movement: get it done, take it to the streets.

The 1968 uprisings in Paris were but one example of protest activity happening at the time: anti-Vietnam protests in the US and demonstrations against the Franco dictatorship in Spain were

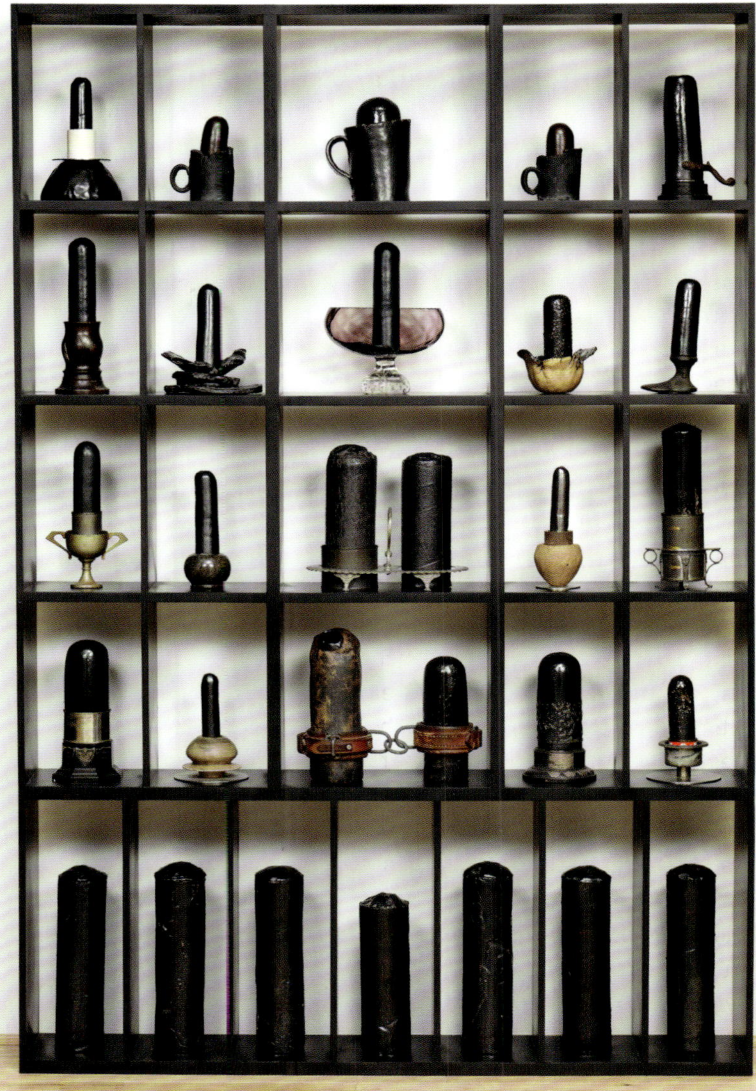

happening concurrently, while the Black Panther movement was gaining steam in the US, too. There was revolution in the air; it was a time of social and political change. These movements inspired revolutionary art, and art that was protest itself. The art or artist does not have to sit within or engage with particular political movements and humanitarian organisations, but they may still catalyse them; by identifying the unknown or shining a spotlight on particular issues, they are encouraging their remedy.

Donald Locke's *Trophies of Empire* 1972–4 (p.19) is a perfect example of this. Consisting of cylindrical forms of various sizes housed in the compartments of a wooden, shelved cabinet, the complex work questions the idea of commemoration. The title of the work reveals the core investigations of the artist: it implies that the bullet-like objects, which are mounted into a variety of fittings, including a trophy cup and candle holders, have a connection with colonialism and slavery. Locke is inviting us to question whose trophies these may be, what aspects of empire are being commemorated and celebrated, and whether empire is even something to be rewarded or lauded.

In this book, I have explored artworks made by artists as protest, the remnants of protest as art and protest activity as art. The art included reflects some 80 years of protest. Spanning both time and geography, the works address a large number of issues: social, political and environmental – some of which have pulsed through the veins of humanity throughout history.

What I haven't been able to touch on in this book, for the sake of the format, is the duty of the museums as gatekeepers of these powerful works. Many of the works included in this short survey exist or have existed in public spaces, reaching the masses with immediacy and potency. But we – our museums and curators alike – must be aware that cultural institutions are part of the structures of power that protests often seek to undo. In recognising this, museums must do away with neutrality – we all have a lot to learn from the way artists look at the world, and to the future. We cannot rest on our laurels; we must grow, and fight.

The Power of Protest Art

Art is often utopic, operating on the idea of what could have been and what should be; reflecting on the unrealised potentialities of the world by excavating and attempting to learn from the past and proposing new realities. This is one of the true powers art can bring to protest and political action. With art, artists identify an urgency to create that which does not yet exist, and share that vision with the world. Whether joyful celebration, or critique, art must emerge from a challenge to a world that was idly functioning without it; and protest art challenges further. It has the ability to send the world off-kilter. Today's art is a protest against yesterday and a call to arms for tomorrow.

Protest art is a bludgeon. It is designed to wake us up and make us look at the world differently. Events, the subjectivity of history, and narratives that have been taken for granted without question find vivid interrogation through art. Protest is dialogue, and so the power of protest rests not just in the physical objects, but in the thoughts and conversations they provoke. That is the enduring legacy of great protest art.

Works

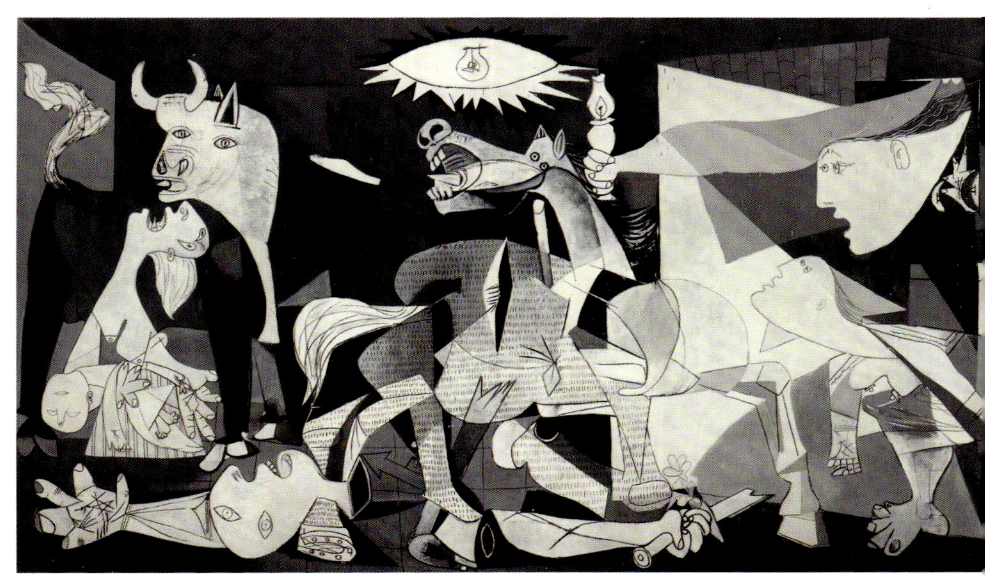

Guernica 1937
Oil paint
on canvas
349.3 × 776.6

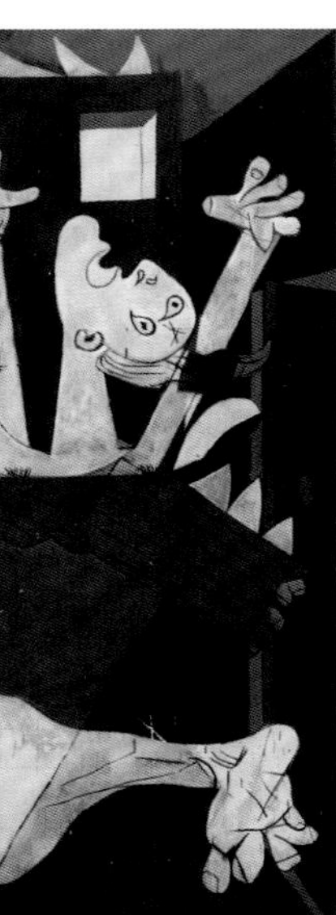

Pablo Picasso once said, 'Art is a lie that makes us realise truth.' Indeed, art should engage with the plight of the time, to remind us of how far we have come and how far we have left to go. To conjure up an image of the Spanish Civil War, one must turn to Picasso's *Guernica*. It is a foremost example of anti-war art. Starting in 1936 (a year before *Guernica* was made) the Spanish Civil War was fought among factions known as the Republicans, loyal to the Spanish government, and the Nationalists, led by a military group under General Francisco Franco. The bombing of the Basque town of Guernica became a critical watershed during the conflict. With the men being on the frontlines, the bombing primarily affected the town's women and children; Picasso homed in on this with his chaotic painting, depicting the terror for all to see. Monochrome, and monumental in size (at approximately 3.5 by 7.8 m, it is one of the largest works Picasso completed), it is tricky for the eye to land on anything for long. His cubist figures are wailing and broken; bombs rain down; a horse screams; feet jut out and hands feel around in desperation. It is a wretched and miserable scene, all but for the lightbulb and the lantern, symbols of hope and, like torches of protest, urging us to keep pushing on. When Picasso's *Guernica* was complete, it toured to engage audiences and raise funds for the Spanish war relief; after all, art lives and breathes when it reaches the masses. Picasso made his art have living value; it depicted the atrocities of war, protested them vehemently and helped safeguard a future for those affected. *Guernica* takes creative licence with the interpretation of events, and in so doing has become an enduring symbol for peace and a warning against the terrors of war, long outliving the conflict it memorialises. In seeing the ugly side of humanity, Picasso reminds us that hell is round the corner if we forget the past.

Pablo Picasso
1881–1973

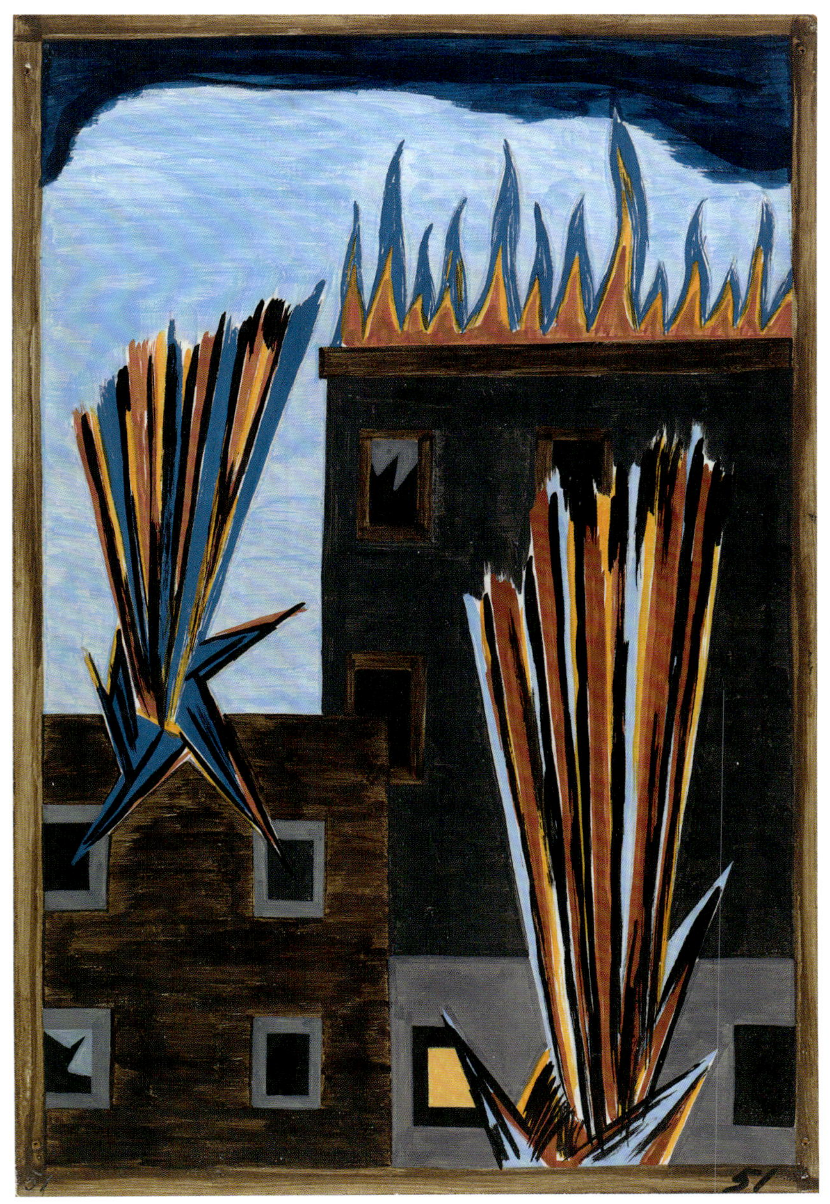

*The Migration
Series, Panel
no. 51* 1940–1
Casein tempera
on hardboard
45.7 × 30.5

Jacob Lawrence's art has long been concerned with the African American experience. His epic *Migration Series* dramatically depicts the Great Migration – the mass movement of over one million African Americans from the rural South to the cities of the North after the First World War – in an inventive narrative, evoking a period that forever altered the social, economic, political and cultural fabric of American society. His powerful and moving imagery handles metaphors of injustice and strife and imbues them with hope and beauty to inspire change. Comprising sixty intimate scenes, the series was born on the brink of the Second World War. During this time America, again, sought the labour of Black people, and so Lawrence devised a cautionary tale of the recent past, and its subsequent disappointments. With a touch of cubist style, the distinctive abstracted and expressive figures play out these warnings in theatrical fashion. The first half of the series illustrates the economic hardship and social injustice of the South, while the second paints a picture of the lives of migrants after they had reached the North. Underpinning *Migration* is the symbol of the journey – the series starts and finishes with an image of a train station – with scenes that switch between hope and despair. From the crowded, squalid corners of the labour camps of the North to its urban slums, Lawrence blurs the lines between the real and the abstract, and conveys the disillusionment of his subjects. The panel illustrated here tells the story of the African Americans who, in looking for better housing moved into new areas, only to have their homes there bombed. The heart-wrenching series concludes with a contrast of class: well-to-do African American residents dressed in furs and top hats next to newcomer migrants in church. The inner workings of each panel are a complexity on their own; together, they form a contemporary altarpiece that recounts the strength of community and the enduring perseverance of African Americans.

Jacob Lawrence
1917–2000

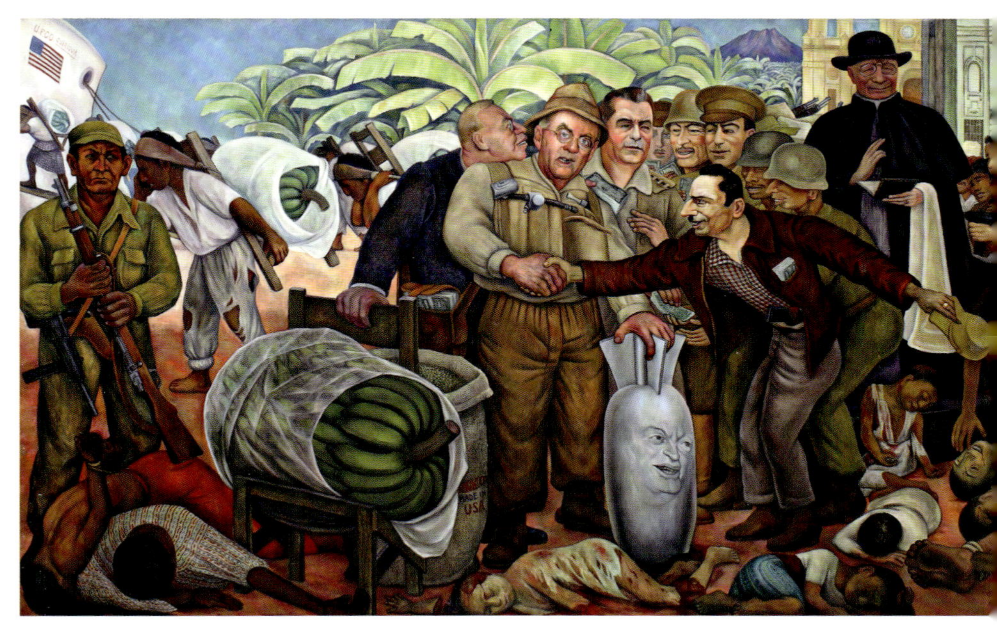

Gloriosa Victoria
(Glorious
Victory) 1954
Oil paint on
canvas 260 × 450

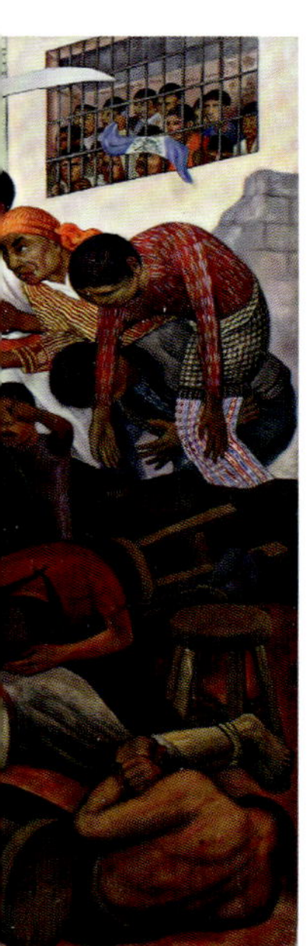

Gloriosa Victoria is a unique example of a 'mural on tour'. The large oil on canvas depicts the 1954 CIA-backed Guatemalan coup d'état. With a punch of protest and the narrative qualities of a Renaissance altarpiece, Diego Rivera illustrates a bleak chapter in humanity, demonstrating the violence against indigenous communities during the Cold War, as well as continuing his career-long dedication to protesting capitalism. Around this time, Mexico was going through a revolution and Rivera became famous for his public murals depicting the changes taking place around him. In *Gloriosa Victoria* he employs his post-cubist style to illustrate the busy scene. The herd of rosy faces in the middle details the American envoy; peachy and a little round from the gluttony of capitalist America. The Guatemalan military cooperate with the Americans, the latter of whom are lighter in skin colour, representing the social whitening and racial mobility Guatemalan officials were afforded. In this rendering, Rivera paints the officials as traitors, who are using the tumultuous situation to improve their own lives instead of those of 'the people'. The Guatemalan people are shown as soldiers or peasants, apart from the man in the centre, with his slick brown leather jacket and a wad of cash in his pocket. His pistol is clean, yet there is a bloody massacre unfolding – his bribe symbolises his condoning of violence, which is veiled ineffectively with the guise of innocence. In fact, there is money everywhere, from inside the satchel of the director of the CIA to the pocket of the Guatemalan. Rivera's warning against greed and power toured Eastern Europe in 1956 before going missing. It was later discovered rolled up in a store room at the Pushkin State Museum of Fine Arts in Moscow, Russia, in 2006. Rivera's social realism was propaganda as protest; he filled Mexico with his ideas and fought for what he believed in, one wall at a time.

Diego Rivera
1886–1957

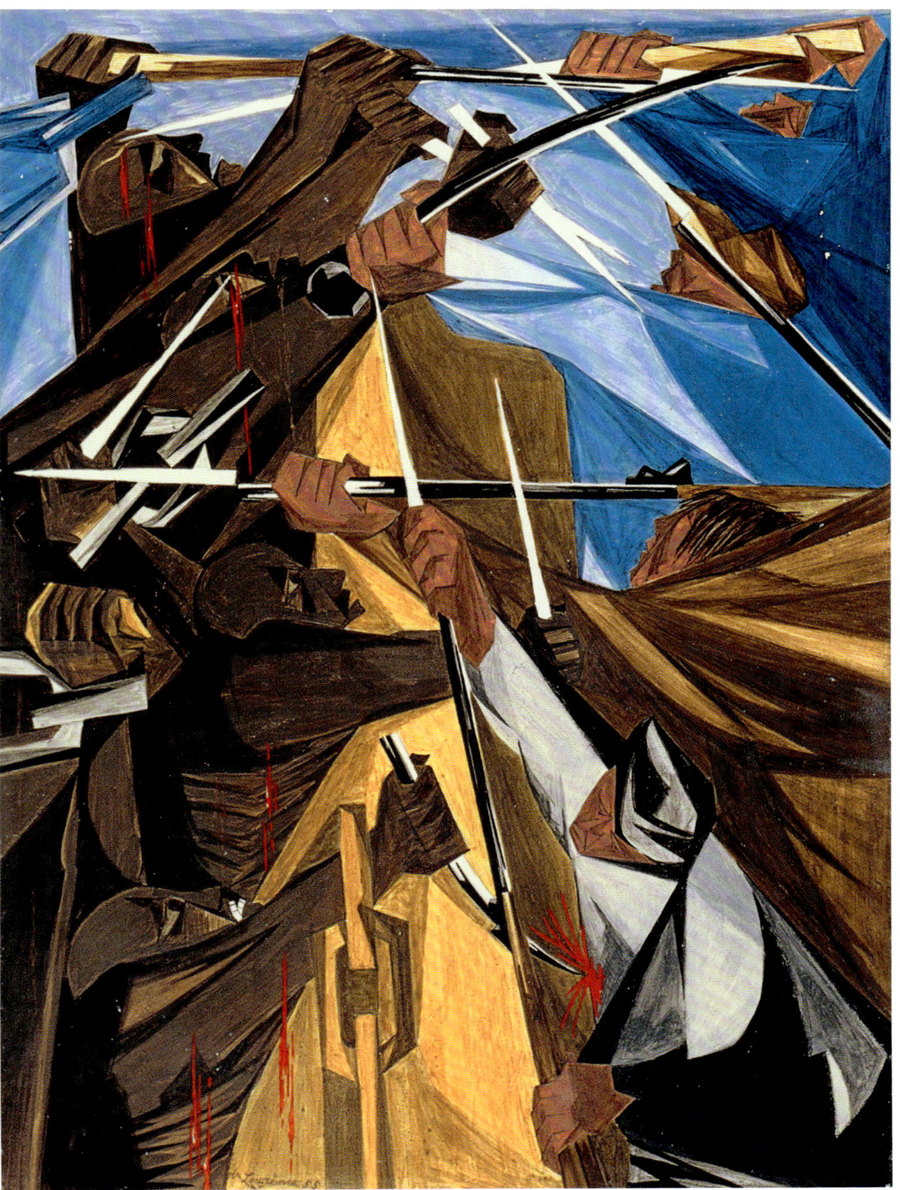

This series of paintings is one of the most evocative ever created by the American modernist Jacob Lawrence, despite it having seldom been seen. 'Who made America great?' is one of the many questions asked by the artist, who, in searching for bits of history that have been pushed to the corner, uncovers a struggle for racial identity. The series takes on the momentous ambition of depicting significant moments in Black history, from European colonisation to the First World War and bringing to life, in the artist's words, 'the struggles of a people to create a nation and their attempt to build a democracy'. Thirty panels, showing historical events from between 1775 and 1817 – from Patrick Henry's famous liberty speech to westward expansion – were completed, and highlight that America, like most countries, has rarely had a moment not faced with struggle. In the panel shown here, titled *'We have no property! We have no wives! No children! We have no city! No country! —petition of many slaves, 1773'*, we see a visualisation of the petition for freedom made by an enslaved man, self-identified only as 'Felix', to the governor of the Province of Massachusetts Bay and its House of Representatives on 6 January 1773. The series was painted at the height of the Cold War, amid Joseph McCarthy's Red Scare (concerning the threat of communism), which also came along with landmark civil rights actions, notably the 1954 Brown v. Board of Education of Topeka Supreme Court ruling that reckoned with the desegregation of public schools. During these tumultuous times Lawrence elevated the experiences of women and people of colour in a jarring cubist-expressionist style. His visual reckoning with the shadowy corners of contention inherent in all histories, but focused bravely on one, is boldly prescient and ahead of its time. Lawrence set down the gauntlet for a complete history. As we confront contemporary issues of racial justice and national identity, we should look again to Lawrence's *Struggle* to pull us through.

Jacob Lawrence
1917–2000

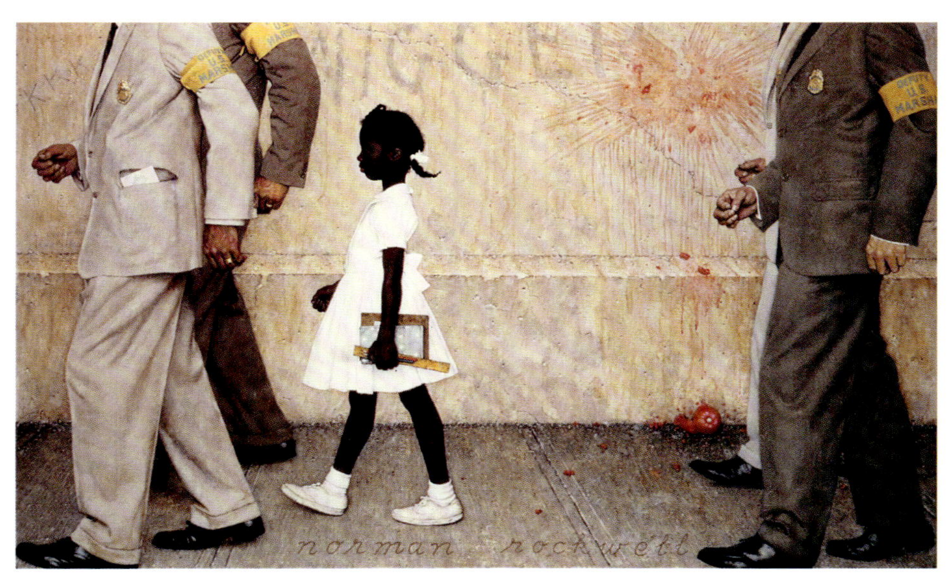

norman rockwell

*The Problem
We All Live
With* 1963
Oil paint
on canvas
91.4 × 147.3

This painting is one of the most iconic images of the civil rights movement in the United States. Painted by Rockwell in 1964, the canvas focuses on the innocence of a young Ruby Bridges, a six-year-old African American girl walking to William Frantz Elementary School. Once we pan out from the guiltlessness of a child in a white dress, the context dawns on the viewer as the peculiar presence of suited white men disturbs the scene. It is 14 November 1960, during the New Orleans school desegregation crisis, and because of threats of violence to the young girl, who is due to attend her all-white public school, she is escorted by four deputy US marshals. As the context is being digested, the word NIGGER in the faintest glinting silver of graffiti on the wall behind her springs from the composition, as do the letters KKK. The splatter of a thrown tomato looks like blood dripping down the wall, hinting at the growing presence of white protestors beyond the confines of the canvas. It is a direct unveiling of the inner workings of the prejudiced mind, where even the innocence of youth is not safe.

The painting was originally published as a centrefold in the 14 January 1964 issue of *Look* magazine. (Rockwell had previously worked for the *Saturday Evening Post* but ended his contract due to its policy of only showing Black people in service industry jobs in its pages.) In this work Rockwell revolts against racism and injustice, while also calling for moral decency. He received praise for the work, but was also accused of betraying the 'white race'. This is testament to the power of the painting, which, in 2011, found its place outside the Oval Office of President Barack Obama. Rockwell pursued his course with fervour, despite irate opinion. In 1965, in M*urder in Mississippi*, he illustrated the killings of civil rights workers in Philadelphia and Mississippi, and in 1967, in *New Kids in the Neighbourhood (Negro in the Suburbs)*, he chose children, once again, as his subjects to illustrate desegregation in the suburbs.

Norman Rockwell
1894–1978

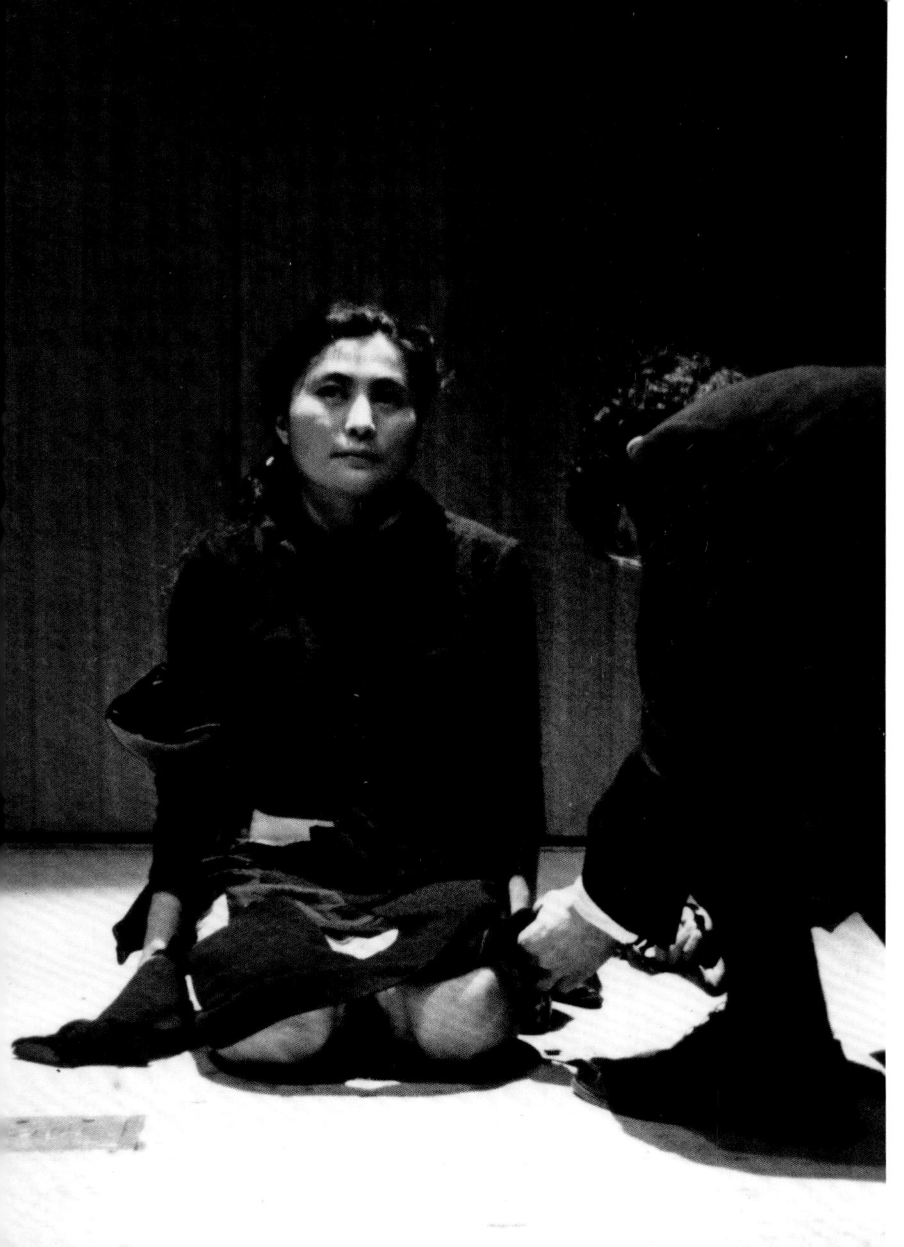

In *Cut Piece*, Yoko Ono sits alone on stage, dressed in her best suit, with a pair of scissors in front of her. This work, first staged on 20 July 1964 at Yamaichi Concert Hall in Kyoto, Japan, invites the audience to approach Ono and use the scissors to cut off a small piece of her clothing, which they could keep. What would you do? Some approached with caution, snipping little corners of her sleeve or skirt, others came in boldly, attacking her bra and blouse.

There have been multiple readings of Ono's stoic performance; she remained motionless and expressionless throughout, until she called the performance to a close. In offering her body to the world – to cut, tear and expose as they please – she also questioned how women are seen, approached and used. The intimate encounter between the artist and the audience becomes a symbol of (female) passivity and vulnerability, while the latent potential for sexist and racist violence and for destructive desire becomes increasingly apparent. This feminist reading casts the audience as test subjects to understand how, given the opportunity, humanity treats women. Walking up onto a concert hall stage and snipping the clothes from a thirty-one-year-old, passive female artist is a provocative act. In participating, Ono is implicating the viewer in the act of unveiling her female body as well as casting the body as object. Notably, in 2003, the year US troops invaded Iraq and almost forty years after she first performed *Cut Piece*, Ono re-enacted the work in Paris as a call for peace and a demonstration against the political climate after 9/11. She asked the audience to send the cut pieces of her clothing to a loved one as a sign of reconciliation. In this move she gave a second meaning to her protest, using attacks on her body to decry conflict.

Yoko Ono
b.1933

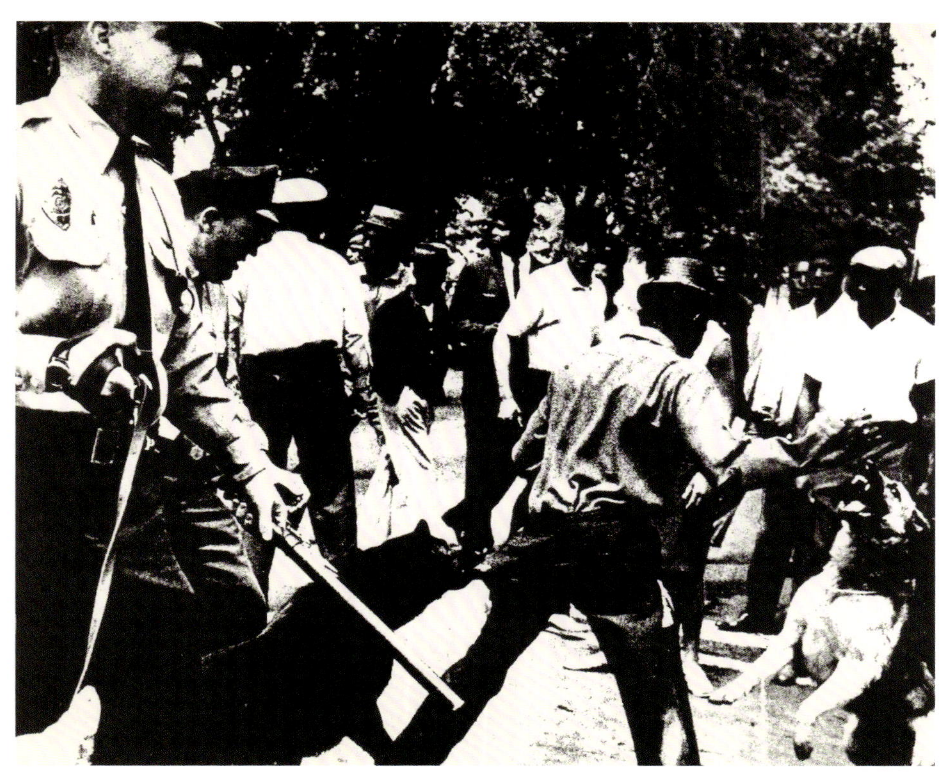

Warhol's *Birmingham Race Riot* epitomises pop art's political cause. The work was inspired by the non-violent action by civil rights demonstrators who sought to end racial segregation in Birmingham, Alabama. The term 'race riot' was commonly used to describe the uprising at the time, but it is important to accurately define the events as protest. In his screenprint, Warhol presents an image of a police dog attacking an African American man. The original photograph, taken by Charles Moore and published as part of a photo essay in *Life* magazine in 1963, brought the oppression of African American citizens and police brutality to the fore. In his essay Moore also showed young Black protestors being fire-hosed, which shocked and moved the American public in the same way that images of the daily atrocities committed against protestors and innocent Black civilians, circulated on social media, do today. In thinking of the resurgence of the Black Lives Matter movement, prompted by the murder of George Floyd in summer 2020, the work is harrowing proof that not much changes after all. Warhol reused this image in *Race Riot* 1964 – a four-panel painting tinted in red, white and blue, and which replicates the high-contrast monotone quality of a newspaper – to show the dark underbelly of the American Dream; a theme he repeatedly embraced and critiqued and which, in reproducing such imagery as art, sought to question how shock is received within the hallowed hall of the gallery space.

Andy Warhol
1928–87

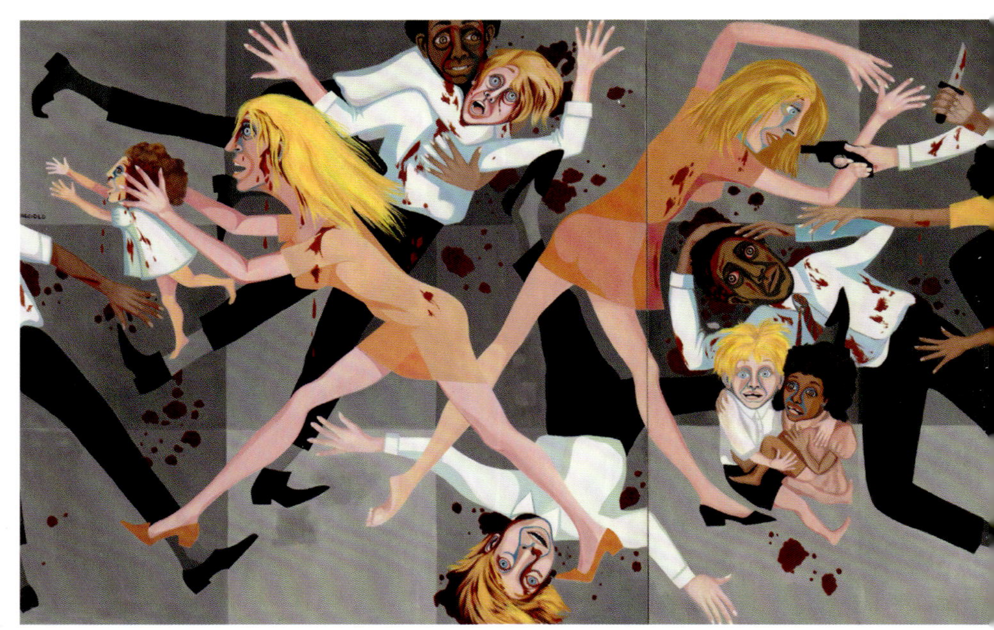

*American People
Series #20: Die*
1967, Oil paint
on canvas; two
panels 182.9 ×
365.8

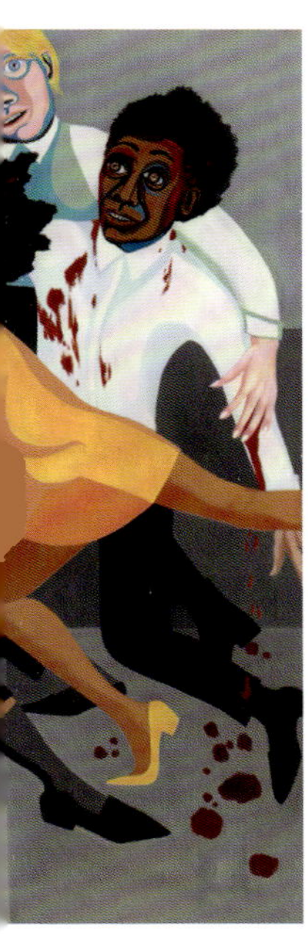

This painting is hard to look at, but no harder than the reality it depicts. Ringgold wants you to be upset. You don't paint people fighting, blood spilling and children cowering without an intent to stir feeling. By offering us her eyes, this work is supposed to agitate and induce a bilious response; one that makes us stop, think, reflect and revaluate how we see the world.

Ringgold's *American People Series* confronts race relations in the United States in the 1960s, and this mural-scale painting concludes the series, culminating violent chaos with the riots that were erupting throughout the country, as fighting in the streets and undocumented killings of African American people took place with regularity. Such scenes seldom featured on television or in the media, and so Ringgold sought to give the crisis an image. Like the sharp chaos of Picasso's *Guernica* 1937 (p.24) and Jacob Lawrence's *Struggle: From the History of the American People* 1954–6 (p.30), Ringgold's dynamic composition shows an interracial group of men, women and children, mid-air and riled up. Blood is drawn and spatters evenly; the struggle touches everyone. All the figures are dressed well, in business attire, holding the well-to-do professional class accountable and showing that, at the core of the fight, is a determined struggle by the middle classes to ensure that their positions are not usurped. Set against a grey, paved sidewalk, a frequent backdrop in this series, its urbanity underlying the subject matter's contemporaneity, children huddle in the centre; the innocent victims of the violence.

The struggle was going on then, and it happens now. The fight doesn't end; it just metamorphosises. Ringgold abstracts this struggle into clear truths that reveal its timelessness. Thus, the painting is an abstraction detailing what the riots were really about – race and class. It calls attention to that fact there is still much work to be done, individually and collectively.

Faith Ringgold
b.1930

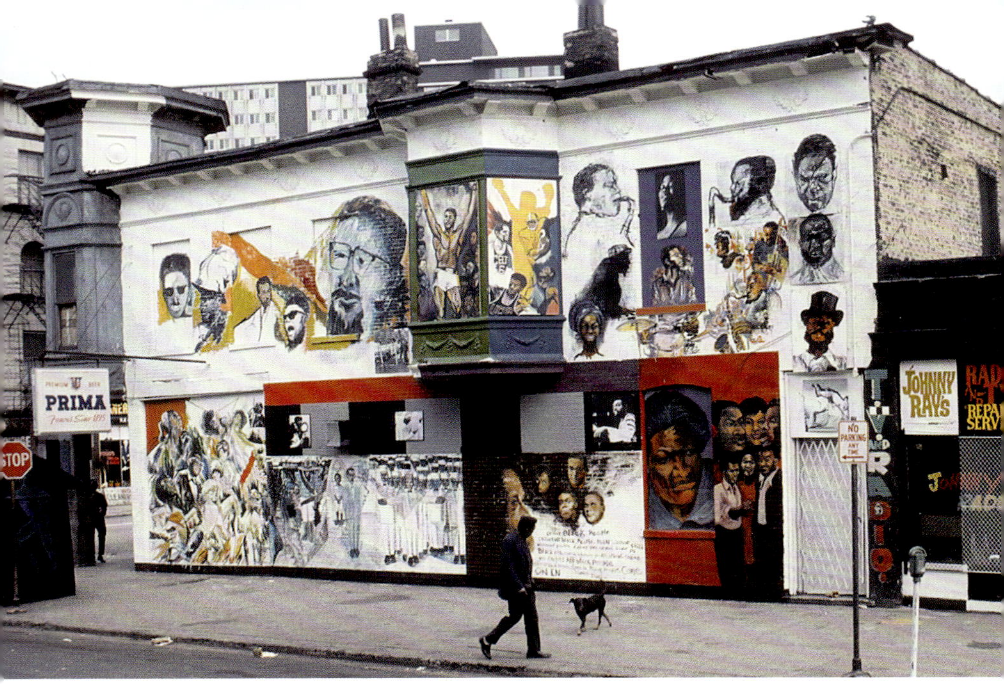

Wall of Respect
1967, Mural
c.600 x 800

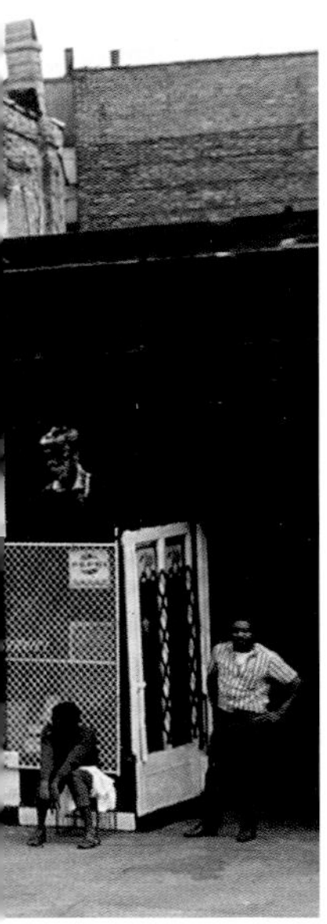

Wall of Respect is a group mural conceived by William Walker, a member of the Organization of Black American Culture (OBAC), a vibrant artistic collective that emerged in the South Side of Chicago in 1967 and which was active during the US civil rights movement.

The giant, 6 × 18-m mural presided on the wall of a derelict tavern and the general theme was designed by local student Sylvia Abernathy and executed by artists from OBAC's Visual Artists Workshop. The ambitious scheme divided the existing features of the building into seven categories – Statesmen, Athletes, Rhythm and Blues, Religion, Literature, Theatre, Jazz – to delineate different types of heroes, with Malcolm X, Muhammad Ali, Aretha Franklin, Nat Turner, Gwendolyn Brooks, Cicely Tyson and Miles Davis all rubbing shoulders alongside emotive scenes of slavery.

Wall of Respect demanded attention, with each section executed in the respective artist's style. As history accelerated, and the civil rights movement unfolded, amendments and new scenes were called for – the mural becoming an exciting example of in-situ picture-making. If painting history in real time, in a time of reckoning such as this, was feat enough, the wall became an important place for political gatherings; a pilgrimage site for tourists and activists and a platform for Black creativity, as musicians, dancers and poets all performed at the site. It was a modern-day Roman Forum, a place for politics to activate. It did what all good public art should do: protest for a better future. Though the mural was short-lived, its contention is part of the legacy of mural-making as social activation and has inspired mural movements around the world. Parts of the wall were vandalised; the body of a murdered community member, Brother Herbert, was left propped against it; and after it had been damaged by fire the city's officials deemed the site unsafe. The contested nature of the site seemed to mirror the politics it depicted, if only people were kept as sacred as buildings.

Various artists

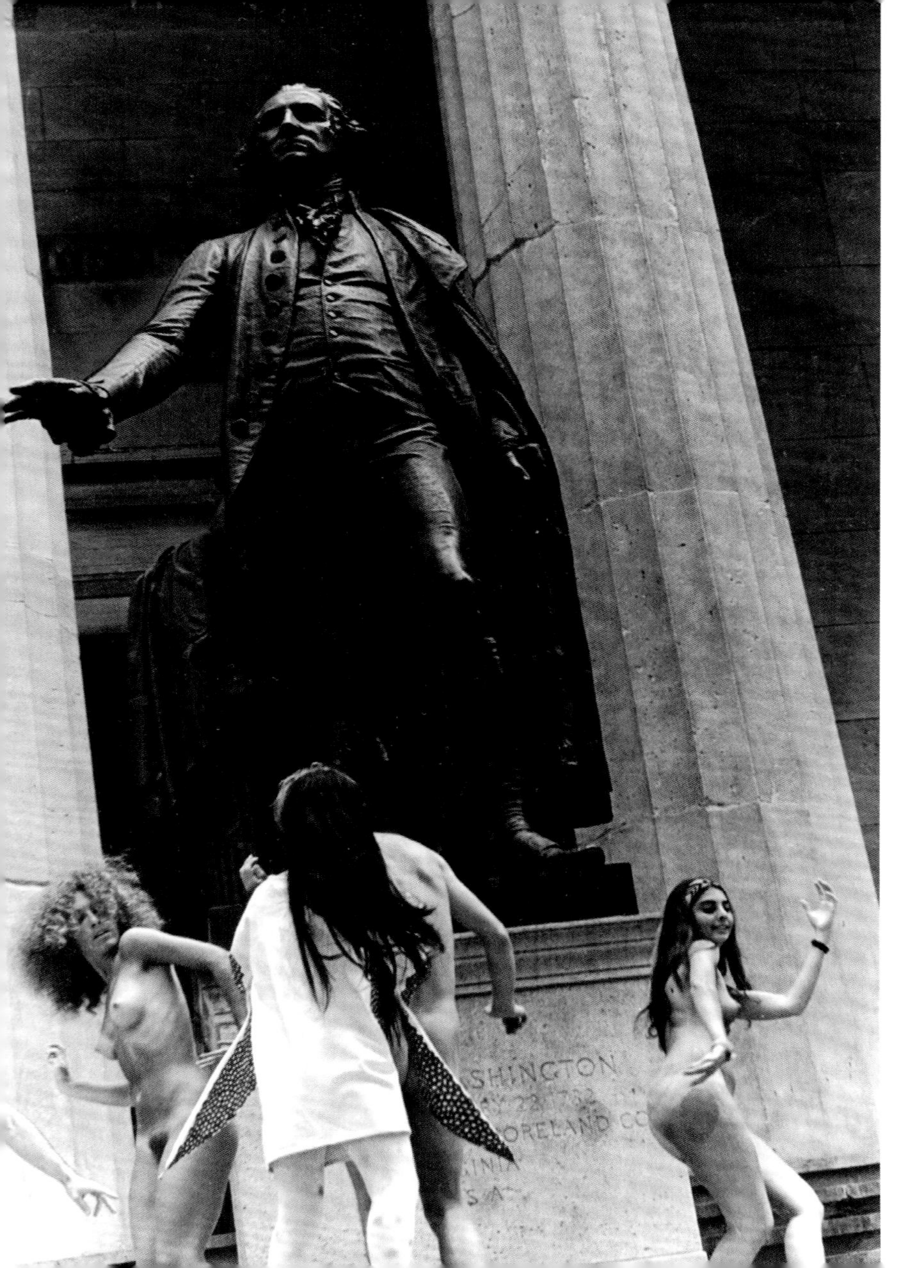

SHINGTON
ORELAND C
INIA
SA

Known for her immersive polka-dot installations, Kusama embraced political revolt of her own styling in the 1960s, by staging demonstrations in New York against the Vietnam War. These protests, named *Anatomic Explosions*, sought to counteract violence with 'love-ins' and naked, polka-dot body-painting happenings. In her *Anatomic Explosion* staged in 1968, naked dancers frolicked opposite the New York Stock Exchange. In the part-press release, part-manifesto for the occurrence, she claimed, 'The money made with this stock is enabling the war to continue. We protest this cruel, greedy instrument of the war establishment.' Swinging between participatory protest culture and mystical ceremony, the release stated 'Burn Wall Street. [...] OBLITERATE WALL STREET MEN WITH POLKA DOTS. OBLITERATE WALL STREET MEN WITH POLKA DOTS ON THEIR NAKED BODIES. BE IN ... BE NAKED, NAKED, NAKED.' The gyration to bongo drums, and spray-painting of blue polka dots onto naked bodies, got the attention of police fast, but that did not stop further performances by the self-proclaimed 'modern Alice in Wonderland'. Her theatrical demonstrations painted a technicoloured fantasy of protest culture, with optimism at the core of its politics. Kusama then went on to pen an 'OPEN LETTER TO MY HERO, RICHARD M. NIXON', where she writes: 'Our earth is like one little polka dot, among millions of other celestial bodies, one orb full of hatred and strife amid the peaceful, silent spheres. Let's you and I change all that and make this world a new Garden of Eden ... You can't eradicate violence by using more violence.' After returning to Japan, Kusama created a series of anti-war collages which featured distressing images from news magazines, overlaid with watercolour and pastel. Later, in 1995, she commemorated the victims of the atomic bomb in Hiroshima in a large triptych. *Revived Soul* is removed of colour, and comprises abstracted vertical bands of black and white that resemble trees, all covered in polka dots.

Yayoi Kusama
b.1929

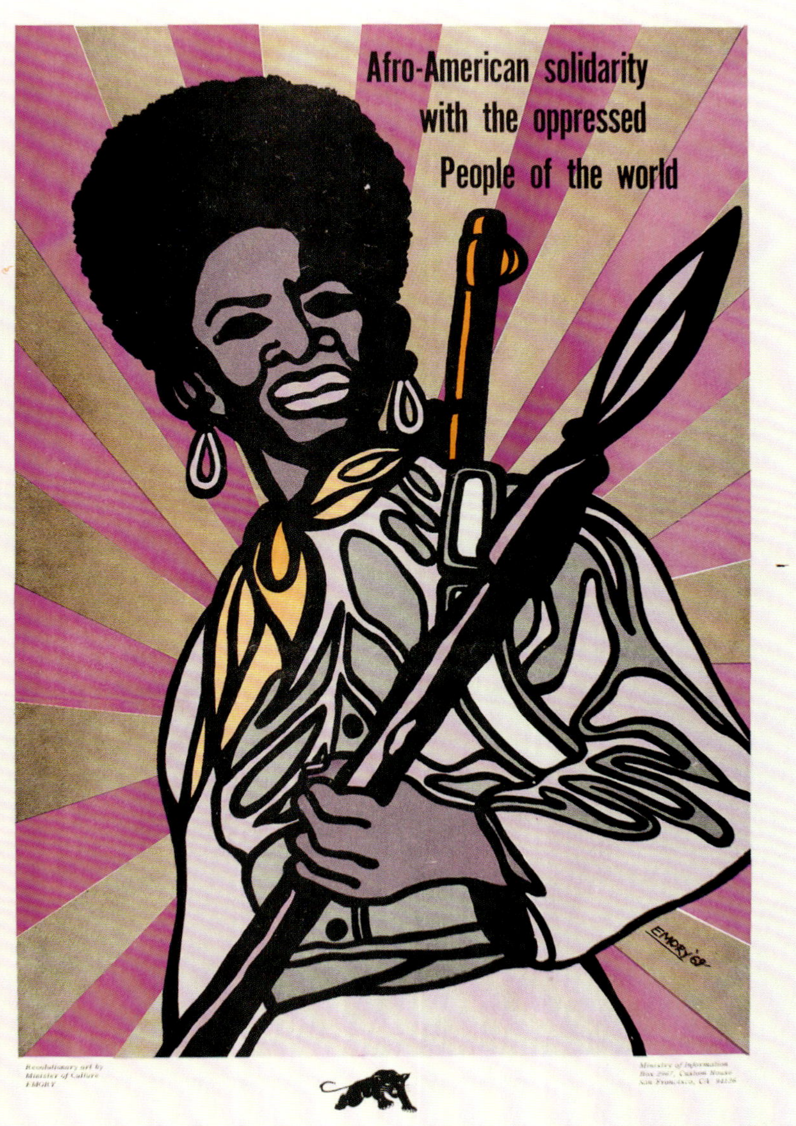
Afro-American solidarity
with the oppressed
People of the world
EMORY '68
Revolutionary art by
Minister of Culture
EMORY
Ministry of Information
Box 2967, Custom House
San Francisco, CA 94126

In 1980 the final issue of *The Black Panther* newspaper was published. Established in 1967, the paper boasted a readership of 400,000 at its peak. Its *modus operandi* was to advance the social and political interests of the Black Panthers; to inspire, recruit and inform supporters. At its helm, these directives were carried out by the art of the Black Panther Minister of Culture, Emory Douglas. Douglas, a former graphics student, joined the group in 1967, at the age of twenty-two. He made the often overlooked and oppressed everyday Black citizen the focus of his bright and bold imagery and his designs for pamphlets and posters, and through the newspaper transcribed the party's ideology into a visual iconography that eventually defined its identity. In this image, the purple-black female is transformed into a heroine, with dusty and bright pink sunburst rays emanating power and defiance. Wielding a spear, and with a gun and the powerful text 'Afro-American solidarity with the oppressed People of the world', this is an example of a style that became synonymous with the party. Clear and to the point, the poster resonates with the struggle between the oppressed and the oppressor and depicts a hopeful saviour – the every-man and -woman. This fundamental rhetoric, with its immediate relatability, was directed at the 'lumpen' (working class) audience, as the Panthers (following Karl Marx's term *Lumpenproletariat*) nicknamed them. Thus, Douglas's polemic figures, outlined in thick, black ink, leave little room for misreading. *Afro-American Solidarity* conveys the force of revolution to those who need it.

Emory Douglas
b.1943

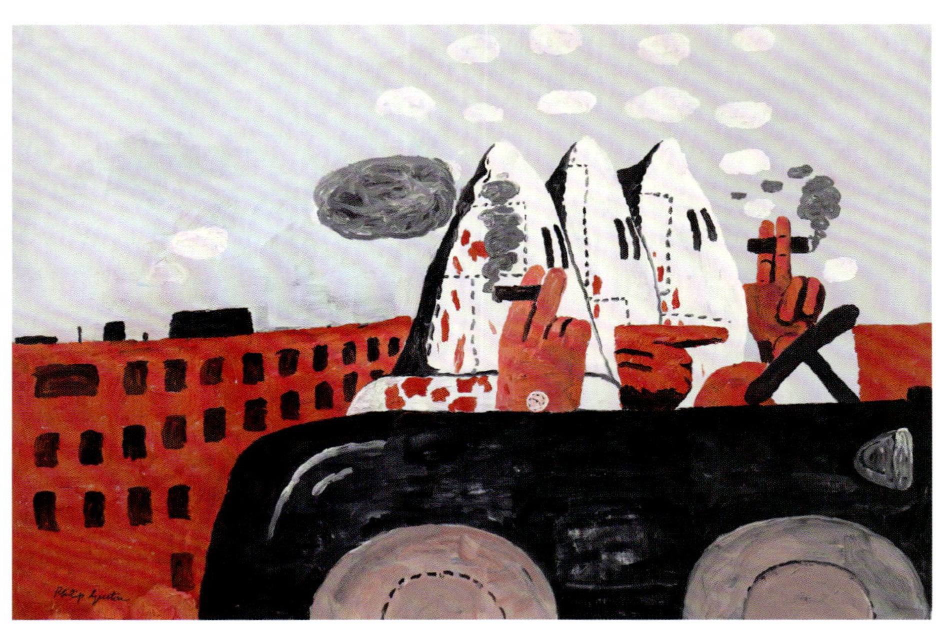

Philip Guston's provocative Ku Klux Klan pictures make us look at the face of evil and laugh at their ridiculosity. Wildly political, after working with abstract expressionism, he returned to figurative representation with a scathing and satirical outlook. One such example is his fresco from the 1930s made in collaboration with Reuben Kadish, *The Struggle Against Terrorism*, which depicted Nazi and Ku Klux Klan brutality. Prompted by the violence and civil unrest in the late 1960s, Guston felt compelled to tell a story of an America 'run afoul of its democratic promise'. The result was the Klan paintings. *Riding Around* depicts cartoon-like figures driving in cars – wearing Ku Klux Klan robes. Guston's paintings make us think hard. In the midst of the Vietnam War, the Black Power and civil rights movements, they are a declaration that Black Lives Matter. Fully immersed in a political reality, the Klan, who have served bilious attacks for so long, look markedly foolish and pathetic in the banality of the day-to-day. Guston weakens them, turning them into bouncy, ghost-like cartoon characters. In their simplistic caricaturing, we are called to laugh in the face of evil – a powerful repositioning of power that still makes us uncomfortable. However, change feels uncomfortable. It gurgles in your belly, it riles you up. Change means protest, hard conversations and silent contemplation – and Guston serves as a poignant catalyst.

Philip Guston
1913–80

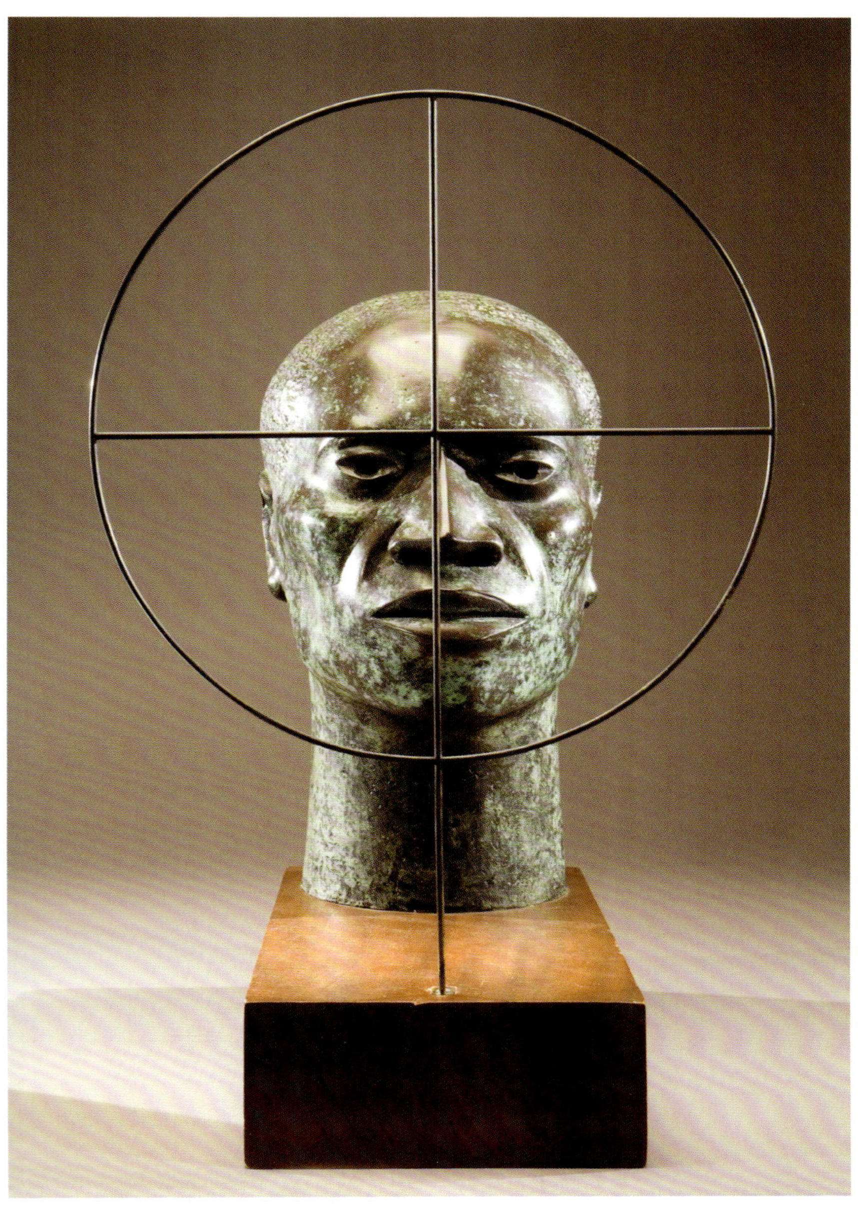

Target 1970
Bronze 50.8
× 35.6 × 55.9

Elizabeth Catlett is one of the few commercially successful and recognised African American women artists of the mid 1900s and is best known for her unabashed challenging of racial injustice and her confidence that art could foster social change. Her sculptures, which frequently confront the most unsettling injustices to African Americans head-on, became symbols of the civil rights movement, as she blended art and social consciousness to striking and potent effect. *Target*, a sculpture of a Black male head framed by a rifle sight, came after the shooting of Black Panther activists Fred Hampton and Mark Clark by Chicago police officers in December 1969. In this simple reframing of a traditional bust, Catlett is attesting that the African American male experience is fraught with racially initiated violence. The enlarged gun sight centres the face in crosshairs for the viewer – Catlett is pushing injustice right into our face and dares us not to look. She questions our complicity in witnessing injustice and demands that more is done. Catlett's work consistently deals with race and injustice and is at its most forceful in *Target*. The sculpture ages with a seafoam green patina that raises questions about its age, and in so doing, highlights the historical consistency of afflictions against the Black male. With this work Catlett is asking 'When will this end? When will Black people be more than just target practice?'

Elizabeth Catlett
1915–2012

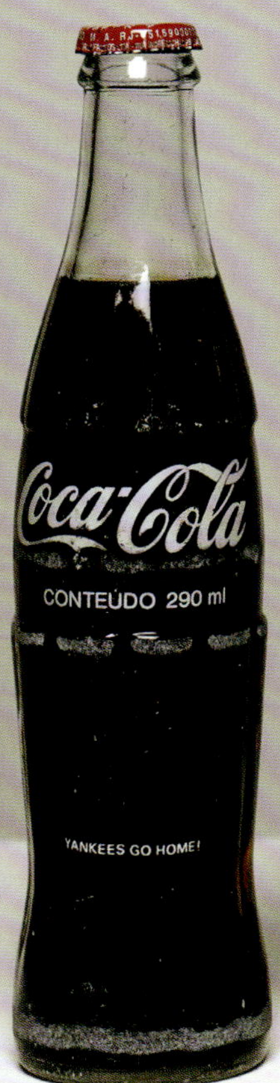

Coca-Cola
CONTEÚDO 290 ml
YANKEES GO HOME!

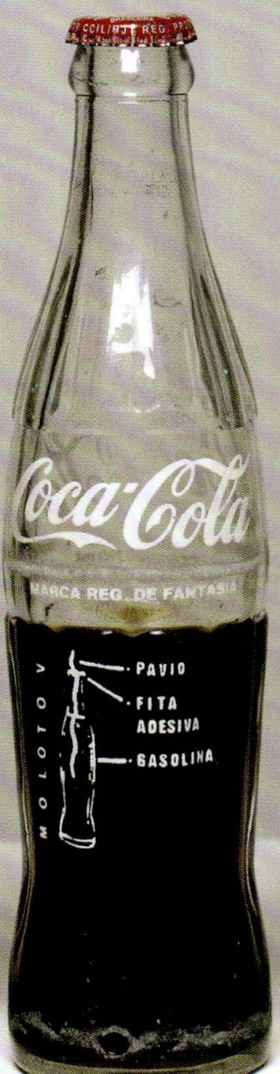

Coca-Cola
MARCA REG. DE FANTASIA
MOLOTOV
PAVIO
FITA
ADESIVA
GASOLINA

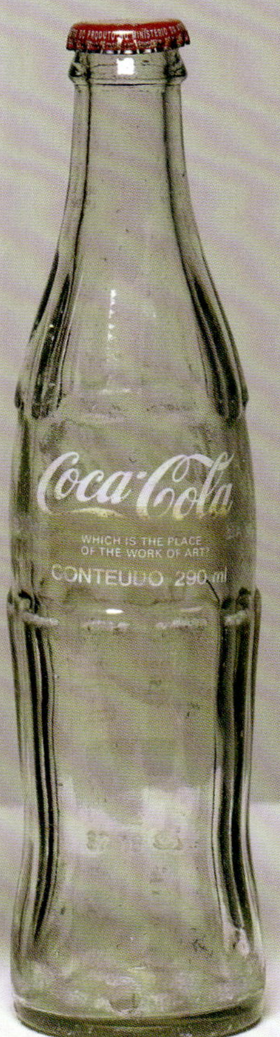

Coca-Cola
WHICH IS THE PLACE
OF THE WORK OF ART?
CONTEÚDO 290 ml

Insertions into Ideological Circuits: Coca-Cola Project 1970
Three glass bottles, three metal caps, liquid and adhesive labels with text
25 × 6 × 6 each

Cildo Meireles's *Insertions into Ideological Circuits: Coca-Cola Project* is proof that protest art works best when it's stealthy. Too often, those who wish to be complacent can turn away their heads from protest. However, what if you present people with something they cannot ignore, and in a place they'd least expect? Meireles did just that, by reconciling his practice with a system for circulating and exchanging information that eschewed centralised control. The system? Coca-Cola bottles. The Brazilian artist removed bottles from circulation and added to them critical political statements and, in one case, even the instructions for making a Molotov cocktail, or petrol bomb, and then put them back into the circuit of exchange. In so doing, phrases such as 'Yankees Go Home' on everyday objects of mass circulation became a powerful revolt, not only against US imperialism but capitalist consumerism, since Coca-Cola was a symbol of both in Brazil in the 1970s. As the bottle empties of the sugary brown fizz, the statements and instructions that were printed in white letters on a transparent label disappear, only to return when the bottle is refilled for recirculation. Fancy some protest with your fizzy pop? Drink too much and you might just change your politics.

Cildo Meireles
b.1948

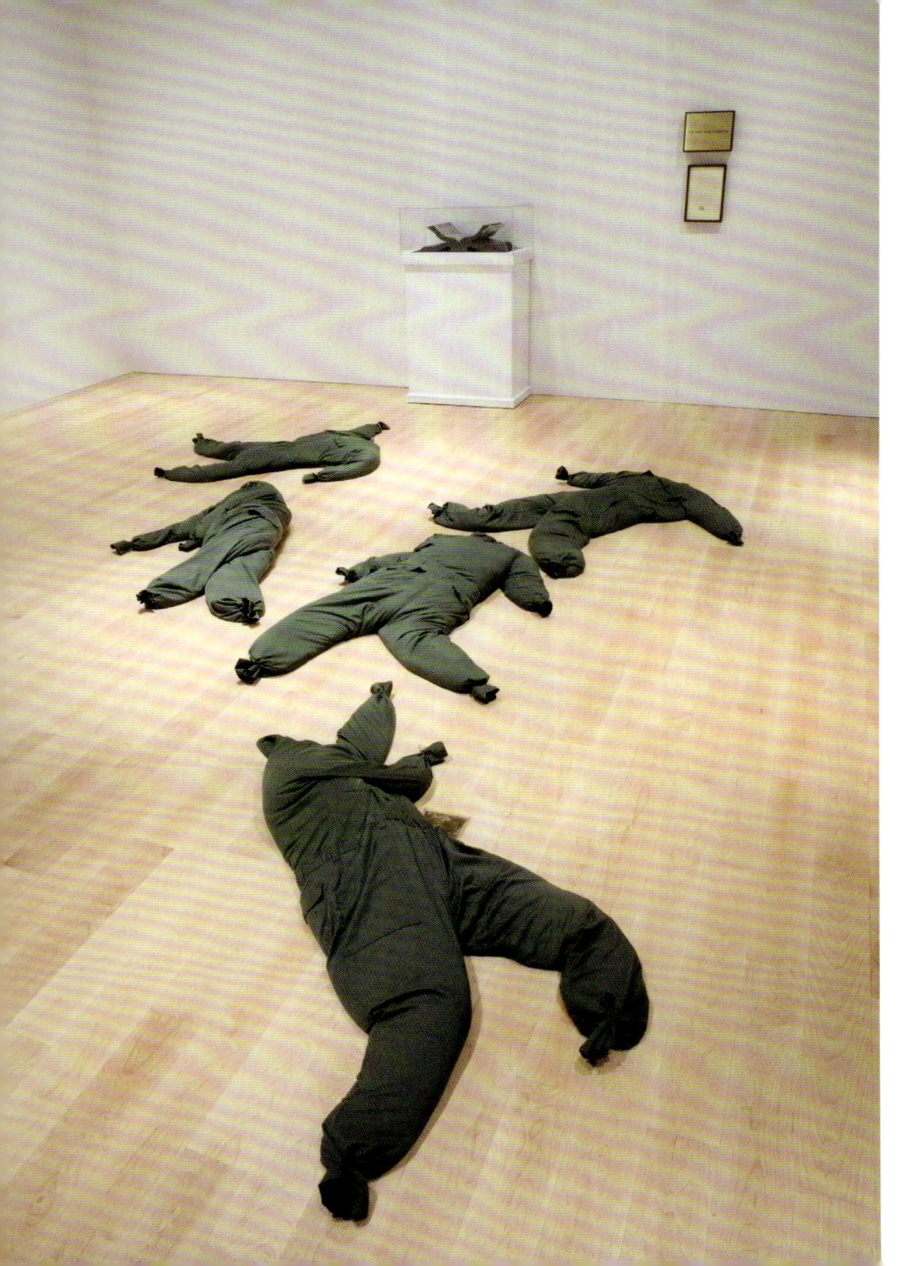

The Non War Memorial
1970, American military uniforms from the Vietnam War period, dirt, seeds, book, podium and plexiglass box
Dimensions variable

The senseless casualties and deaths of the Vietnam War provoked Edward Kienholz to create *The Non War Memorial*. Historically, memorials have commemorated the valiant, the brave and the tragedy of lives lost at war. This memorial does not martyr or glorify death as a necessary part of victory; rather it shoves mortality into your very eyes and dares you to look away. Although never realised, Kienholz's Concept Tableau envisioned 50,000 surplus uniforms filled with dirt to resemble corpses, placed haphazardly around a 30-hectare meadow near Clark Fork, Idaho. As the uniforms broke down, dissipated and degraded, the installation would fade away, with wildflowers emerging and the land returning to normal. Kienholz at once protests war and its romanticisation. He shows the true cost of war and, in this disappearing act, shows how quickly we forget about it.

Edward Kienholz
1927–94

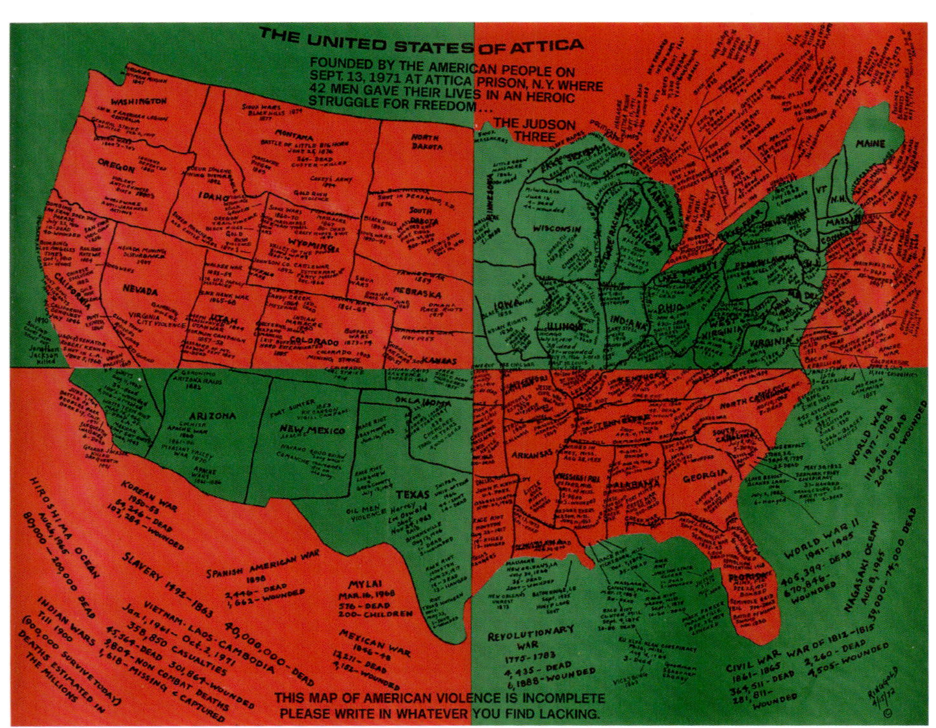

THE UNITED STATES OF ATTICA
FOUNDED BY THE AMERICAN PEOPLE ON SEPT. 13, 1971 AT ATTICA PRISON, N.Y. WHERE 42 MEN GAVE THEIR LIVES IN AN HEROIC STRUGGLE FOR FREEDOM...
THE JUDSON THREE
WASHINGTON
OREGON
IDAHO
MONTANA
NORTH DAKOTA
SOUTH DAKOTA
WYOMING
NEVADA
CALIFORNIA
UTAH
COLORADO
NEBRASKA
KANSAS
ARIZONA
NEW MEXICO
OKLAHOMA
TEXAS
ARKANSAS
MISSOURI
ILLINOIS
IOWA
WISCONSIN
INDIANA
OHIO
MICHIGAN
W. VIRGINIA
VIRGINIA
MISSISSIPPI
ALABAMA
GEORGIA
SOUTH CAROLINA
NORTH CAROLINA
FLORIDA
MAINE
VT
N.H.
MASS
MAINE
HIROSHIMA OCEAN
AUG. 6, 1945
80,000 - 200,000 DEAD
INDIAN WARS
TILL 1900
(900,000 DEATHS ESTIMATED IN THE MILLIONS
DEATHS SURVIVE TODAY?
KOREAN WAR
1950-53
54,246 - DEAD
103,284 - WOUNDED
SLAVERY 1492-1863
40,000,000 - DEAD
VIETNAM - LAOS - CAMBODIA
Jan 1, 1961 - Oct. 2, 1971
358,850 CASUALTIES
45,564 - DEAD 301,864 - WOUNDED
2,804 - NON COMBAT DEATHS
1,618 - MISSING & CAPTURED
SPANISH AMERICAN WAR
1898
2,446 - DEAD
1,662 - WOUNDED
MY LAI
MAR. 16, 1968
576 - DEAD
200 - CHILDREN
MEXICAN WAR
1846-48
13,271 - DEAD
4,152 - WOUNDED
REVOLUTIONARY WAR
1775-1783
4,435 - DEAD
6,1888 - WOUNDED
CIVIL WAR
1861-1865
364,511 - DEAD
281,811 - WOUNDED
WAR OF 1812-1815
2,260 - DEAD
4,505 - WOUNDED
WORLD WAR I
1917-1918
119,516 - DEAD
204,002 - WOUNDED
WORLD WAR II
1941-1945
406,399 - DEAD
670,846 - WOUNDED
NAGASAKI OCEAN
AUG 9, 1945
39,000 - 75,000 DEAD
THIS MAP OF AMERICAN VIOLENCE IS INCOMPLETE
PLEASE WRITE IN WHATEVER YOU FIND LACKING.
RINGGOLD 1972

United States of Attica is a rallying cry for prison reform. In 1971, inmates at Attica Correctional Facility in New York staged one of the most important uprisings for political rights in history. Following the murder of the activist George Jackson at San Quentin State Prison, approximately 1,281 of Attica's 2,200 inmates rioted and took over their prison, taking forty-two members of staff hostage. Authorities acquiesced to the prisoners' demands in the wake of the loss of forty-three lives – ten civilian employees and correctional officers (COs) and thirty-three inmates. Notably, over half of the inmates at the time were Black, and facing racism and brutality from the COs. From 1971 to 1972, Faith Ringgold was moved to commemorate this pivotal uprising by marking the genocides and murders that happened across the United States in the colonial age. This included 2,260 deaths during the Civil War, 264 in the Battle of Little Bighorn and 45,564 lives lost during the Vietnam War. The numbers scream out in bold black text against the green, red and black map, which takes its colours from the Marcus Garvey flag (named after the political leader and civil rights activist, who conceived of the flag as a symbol for Black liberation). The work, relevant still, maps humanity and the lives lost in pursuit of its conservation. Humanity is still at risk from brutality – Ringgold's cry can still be heard.

Faith Ringgold
b.1930

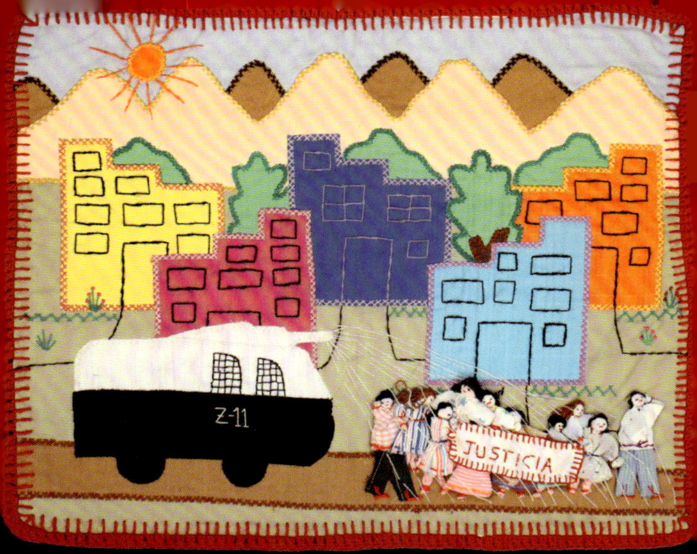

Z-11
JUSTICIA

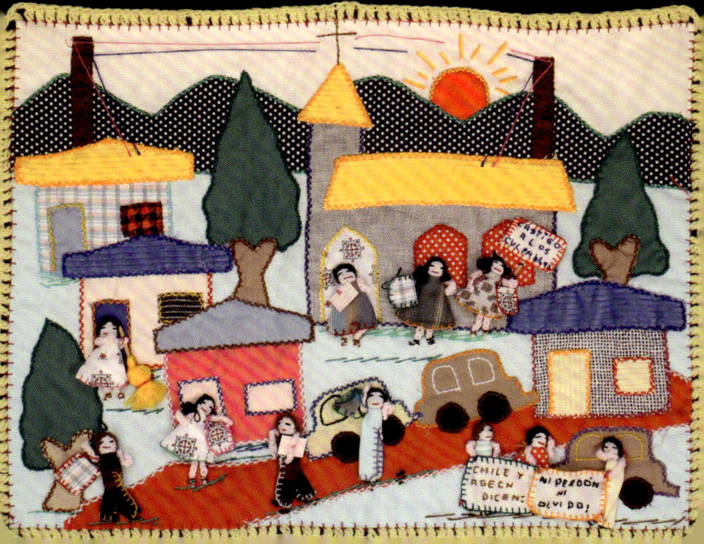

CASTIGO A LOS CULPABLES
CHILE Y AGECH DICEN:
NI PERDÓN NI OLVIDO!

On 11 September 1973 Augusto Pinochet came to power in Chile via a coup d'état. His military government then executed, 'disappeared' or tortured thousands of citizens. Armed with needles and thread, the Association of Relatives of the Detained-Disappeared (AFDD) in Chile started to make *arpilleras*; narrative quilt squares protesting the injustices of the regime. Notably, many of the citizens who disappeared under Pinochet's regime were men, who left female family members in their wake to suffer from economic insecurity as well as emotional turmoil. Handcrafted using scraps of material collected or donated by churches, these moving depictions of personal resilience give insight into the inner workings of the minds of these women, as well as of the female political prisoners who also created *arpilleras* while imprisoned or upon release. Like blog posts or diary entries, the *arpilleras* depicted the bloody side of the regime, detailing instances of disappearances and torture, but also the daily indignities of living under Pinochet. They were also used by prisoners as coded messages for the outside world; to tell their stories of the oppressive, unjust and bloody life under the dictatorship to the wider world and garner the attention of those who could act on their behalf or pass messages to loved ones. These women utilised their 'women's work' for subordinance: to unleash the real narratives to the world and be heard. The *arpilleras* often featured photos, images and names of missing people and stirring expressions such as '*¿Dónde están?*', meaning 'Where are they?' Fashioned from scraps, they have a tactility, which is also enhanced by their 'relief' quality, because they comprise many layers of fabric. The simple, clear lines and forms of the figures are determined, just like those who crafted them. The *arpilleras* are a textile testimony to their makers' tenacity and strength as they struggled for their truth to be heard and for the days under Pinochet to end.

Anonymous artists

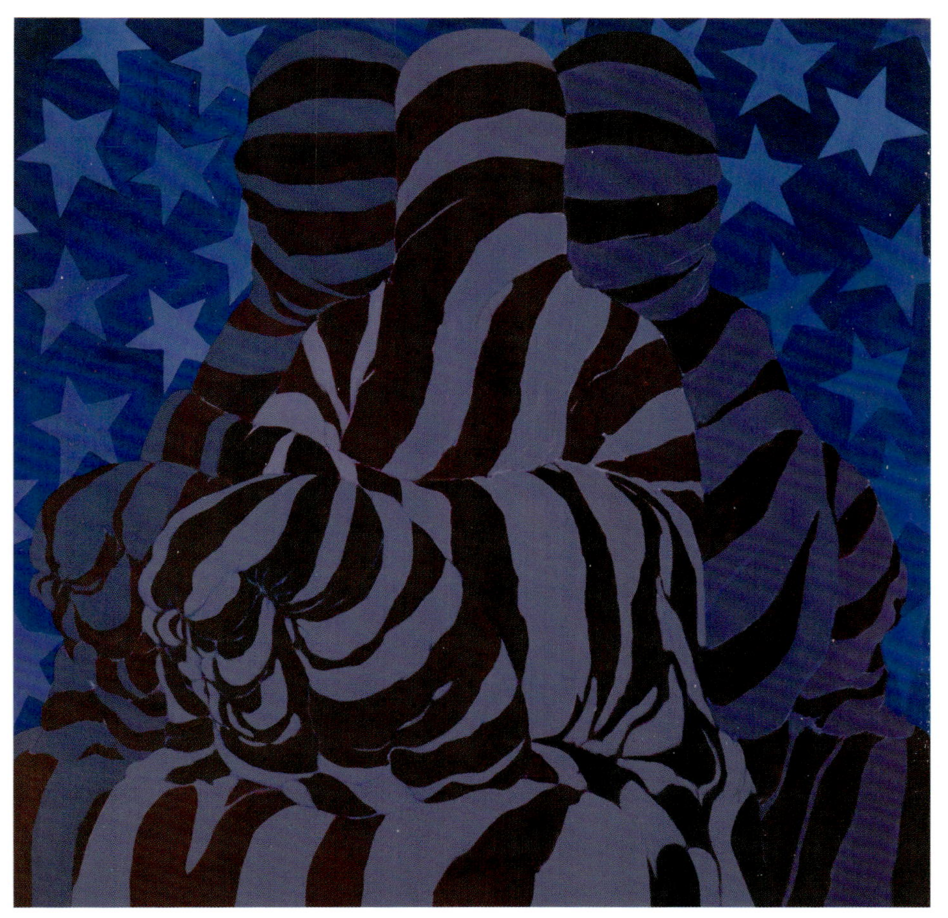

May Stevens had been vehemently against the Vietnam War throughout the 1970s; it inspired her *Big Daddy* series in 1970, and in 1976, on the 200th anniversary of the Declaration of Independence and the year after the US withdrew from Vietnam, she painted *Dark Flag*. In this work Stevens repositions the flag as a symbol of celebration to one of critique and highlights the power it wields as an emblem, both representing patriotism and questioning what Americans should be patriotic about. Stevens was a staunch civil rights activist and feminist, and critical of nationalism. Her *Big Daddy* series, a reaction to her father's racism, sought to challenge white supremacy and its patriarchal foundations, as well as assert how closely issues of race and gender were connected in the Vietnam War. Notably, the three figures in *Dark Flag* drape the flag over themselves like a mourning shroud. Faces covered, they are blinded, silenced and deafened by the flag; transformed into a homogeneous three-in-one form.

The collective rage and mourning over the unlawful deaths of African Americans at the hands of police has sustained for decades, building up with ferocity in recent times. Protected by the fire-blanket flag, we are reminded that not all civilians feel safe, but also that protest and critique can be patriotic. Stevens wishes for a better America and fights for it using its own symbols.

May Stevens
1924–2019

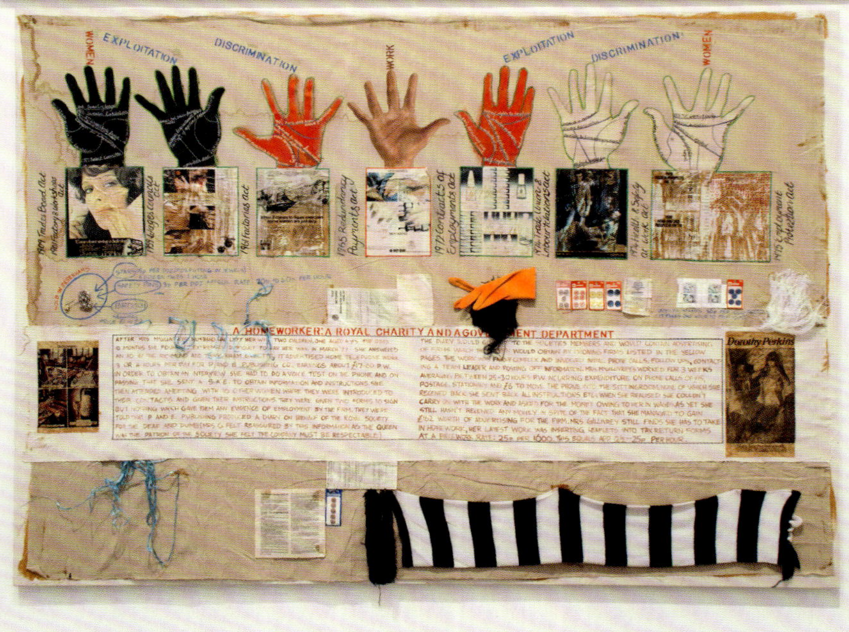

HOMEWORK : HOMEWORKERS
WOMEN
EXPLOITATION
DISCRIMINATION
WORK
EXPLOITATION
DISCRIMINATION
WOMEN
A HOMEWORKER: A ROYAL CHARITY AND A GOVERNMENT DEPARTMENT
Dorothy Perkins

Homeworkers
1977, Acrylic
paint, printed
paper, linen,
graphite,
woollen scarf,
three metal
brooches,
household glove,
twenty-nine
plastic buttons
and wool on
canvas 220 × 244

Margaret Harrison strongly believed that political action and discourse were the sole effective methods for fighting for workers' and women's rights. She began work on *Homeworkers* when the Equal Pay Act came into force in the United Kingdom in 1970, though she had been aware of feminist action since the late 1960s. *Homeworkers* is the central piece in a multidisciplinary project that, through intricate assemblages, encourages the viewer to work through and unpick the various injustices done to women. In it, photographs, interviews and news clippings document the non-unionised women who were doing manual work at home, while the heading, 'HOMEWORK: HOMEWORKERS', stencilled in blue and black, demands your attention. Poignantly, the work itself was laborious to make, as acrylic, graphite and collage are employed to drive the message home. 'WOMEN', 'EXPLOITATION', 'DISCRIMINATION' cry out in blue and red, positioned just above a row of seven hands, which are symbolic of the labour of work. Just below this, advertisements for women's products, mostly cosmetics and beauty items from glossy magazines, are glued to the canvas. Lean further in, and you will see that Harrison has written significant moments in employment legislation, such as '1972 Contracts of Employment act' or '1974 Health & Safety at Work act', as a stark reminder of the poor working conditions that women had to endure before the eyes move further down to stitched buttons, gloves and accessories juxtaposed with selling prices and the number of hours workers invested into their production. Though the work finishes with her manifesto demanding improved conditions for homeworkers, the entire piece is a manifesto in itself. Each meticulously stitched and placed directive forces you to reckon with the truth. Harrison wanted art to do more, and she took it into her own hands.

Margaret Harrison
b.1940

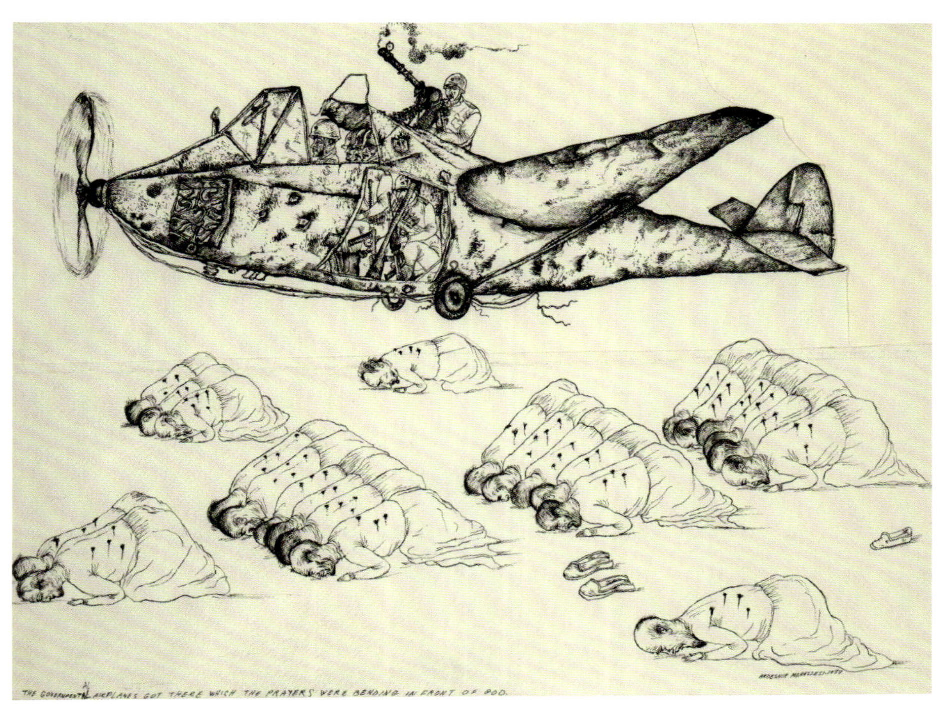

THE GOVERNMENTAL AIRPLANES GOT THERE WHICH THE PRAYERS WERE BENDING IN FRONT OF GOD.

The cultural ecosystems in which protest takes place have great impact on what their protest art looks like. Imagine, for example, protest in a place where freedom of expression is incomprehensible and prohibited, where public outcry is explicitly against the law, or how expression is stifled and, conversely, how it flourishes under a democracy (though, truthfully, this is contestable even under the purportedly free regime of the West). Ardeshir Mohassess's drawings observe power and, with satire and scrutiny, he blends humour and reportage. A cult figure for artists and intellectuals in his home country of Iran, he considered himself a reporter, by way of his political cartoons which, with a scorpion-sharp sting, drew attention to the political wound and called for healing. His career began in his native country, with him drawing in the manner of Saul Steinberg (1914–99), characterfully playful and childlike, and infuriating the shah of the time, Mohammad Reza Pahlavi. Mohassess may have dressed the figures he mocked in Qatar dynasty garb, but people saw through the disguise – his message was clear. His was a full critique of the materialism, injustices and hedonistic hypocrisy of the royal family. His caustic art caused such a furore that the shah put pressure on the publishers and commissions began to dwindle, so Mohassess fled to New York in 1976. However, his relocation to the 'land of the free and home of the brave' did not stop him from taking on Ayatollah Khomeini and and the Muslim leaders in charge following the 1979 revolution. He irked them with equal fervour. His scratchy, inky criticisms leaked ferocity from their nib and knew nothing of censoring or discretion. Decapitations and amputations found their representations by Mohassess's hand. In the work here, we see a ramshackle plane hovering pre-bombardment over a field of civilians, bent down in mid-prayer. Mohassess was compelled to speak out against atrocities and injustices; his drawings don't just speak out, they shout.

Ardeshir Mohassess
1938–2008

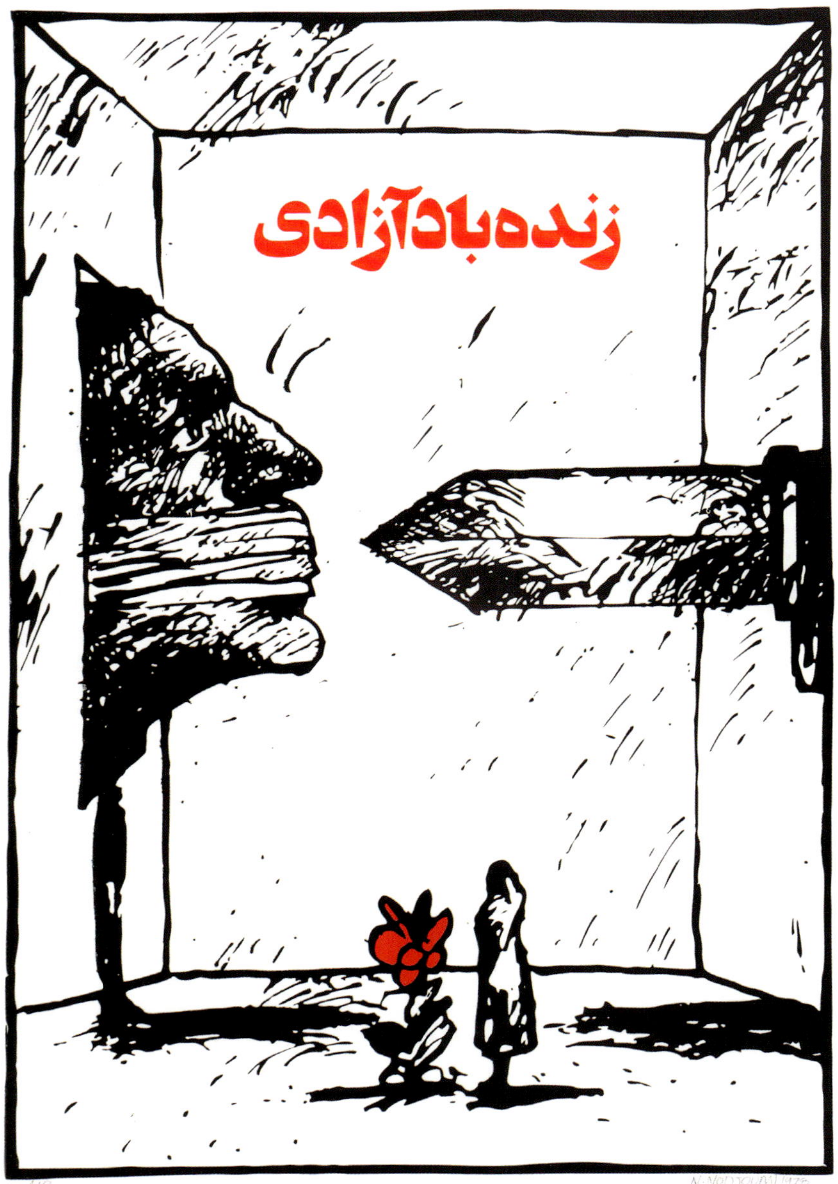

زنده باد آزادی

*Long Live
Freedom* 1978
Screenprint
on paper
100.3 × 69.9

Persian culture has long faced various, extreme injustices, and so the prevalence – in volume and potency – of protest art from Iran in the late twentieth century, challenging past and very present pains, comes with reason. Nicky Nodjoumi arrived in New York from Iran in 1969, where he set to work on a proliferation of political art, much to the detestation of Mohammad Reza Pahlavi, the shah, and his regime. Being forbidden from working or teaching in Iran didn't stop Nodjoumi returning there in 1975 to show his work. He did so annually thereafter, culminating, in tumultuous fashion, with his 1980 solo show at the Tehran Museum of Contemporary Art, which was shut down by Ayatollah Khomeini, who had overthrown Pahlavi in 1979 and pursued the installation of a deeply conservative theocracy. The artist has since turned his eye for satire towards exploring and deriding Iranian and American governance and leadership, among other controversial topics. In *Long Live Freedom*, an early example of his political condemnations, Nodjoumi is protesting the shah's wrongful imprisonment of dissidents. Created for a leftist group, the newspaper-comic-style artwork depicts a bayonet crashing into a prison cell towards a gagged inmate. Nodjoumi's criticisms of power and moral decay caricature the demise of humanity and how quickly people can be subsumed into barbarism.

Nicky Nodjoumi
b.1941

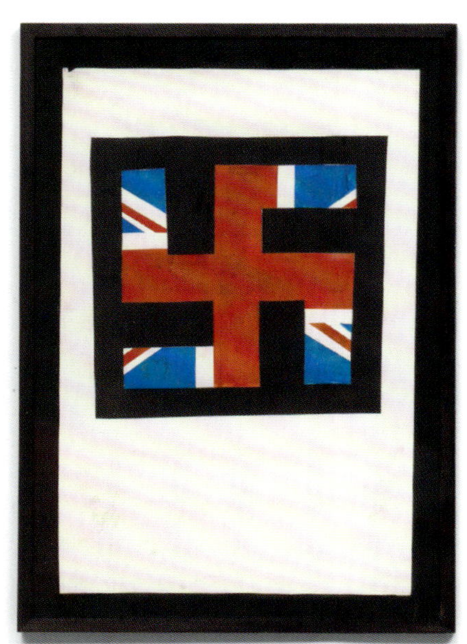
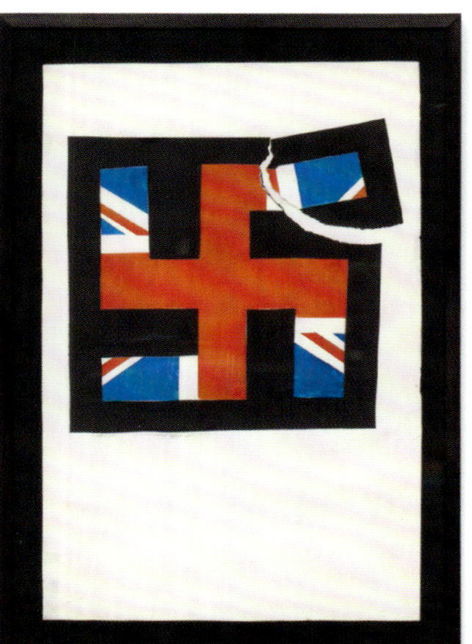
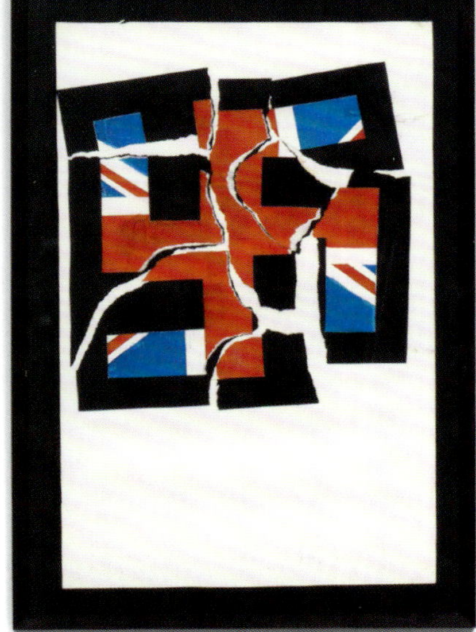
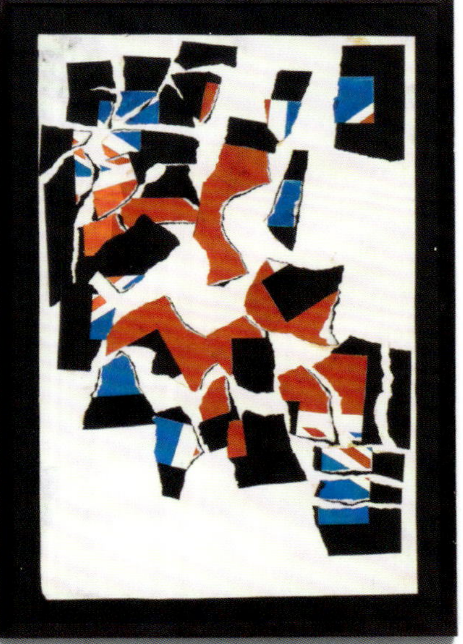

The 1970s saw a prolific increase in nationalist sentiment, encouraged largely by the rapid rise of the National Front in the UK, a political party that advocated for a ban on non-white immigration and for enforced repatriation. *Destruction of the National Front* is a revolt by Eddie Chambers – known for his co-founding in the 1980s of the Blk Art Group, an association of young Black artists raising questions about what Black art was – against the British flag's appropriation by a nationalist racist ideology. Refuting this association of the flag with discrimination, he tore up and reconfigured the image of the Union Jack into a swastika. In so doing, the artist draws attention to the connection between the National Front and Nazism and claims, 'if you're going to be racist … let's show how racist you are'. However, as the fragments scatter, the collage becomes reminiscent of neither flag nor swastika. The dispersal of the flag's fragments becomes symbolic of disillusionment.

Eddie Chambers
b.1960

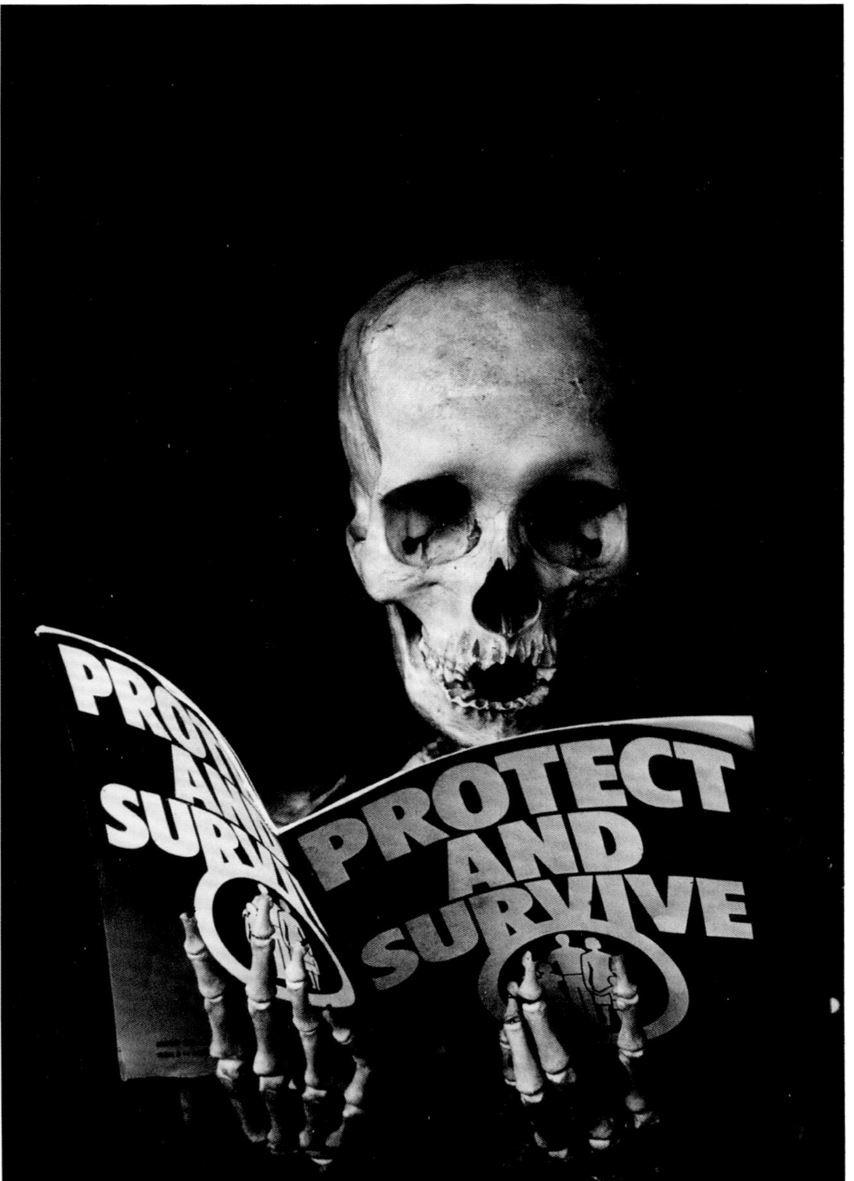
PROTECT
AND
SURVIVE
PROTECT
AND
SURVIVE

Peter Kennard is political dynamite. During the late 1960s he abandoned painting in pursuit of new forms of expression and to free art from bourgeoise sentiment by engulfing it in politics for a wider audience. Kennard has brought his art to the streets – as fly-posters, protest placards and T-shirts in support of organisations such as CND and Amnesty International – since the 1970s. *Protest and Survive* is a sombre and deeply political satirisation of 'Protect and Survive', the nuclear-attack survival guide produced by the UK's Thatcher government during the Cold War. His hard-hitting affront questions her government's propaganda and politics in one macabre swoop. Kennard often employs photomontage; by using the familiarity of something already in circulation, the work is an accessible unveiling of a subliminal 'truth'. Kennard delivers a warning about who to trust, with jutting provocation.

Peter Kennard
b.1949

the unpleasant features of
Imperialism &
«UPRISINGS---SUMMER '81»
EVENING POST
THE 5 Demands
no prison UNIFORM
no work
Free association
Visits
Parcels and REC facilities
Full Remission
CHAPELTOWN
The date:
JULY 13, 1981
babylon burns
liverpool 8
12345
? JUSTICE no more
Equal Rights
b'ham!
st pauls!
peace & love

If There is No Struggle, There is No Progress – Uprisings was made in direct response to the revolts that took place in various cities around England in the summer of 1981. Catalysed, in part, by the social unrest under Margaret Thatcher's government, Burman's work in black, red and white fuses newspaper imagery with chaotic splashes, blotches and etchings, resulting in an artwork that seems almost at war with itself. Part of her *Riot Series*, one of the work's most striking features is the feeling of claustrophobia it incites. Burman's layering of images grates and causes visual tension; the material techniques are overlaid and in conflict, much like the subject matter. Everything is fragmented; images are broken up and put back together again to shift stereotypes and to question, as well as to create, new forms of meaning. 'Liverpool' and 'Chapeltown', referring to the locations of some of the uprisings, are among the words fighting for our attention. Slogans such as '? JUSTICE no more Equal Rights' and 'the unpleasant features of Imperialism' transform the work into a mouthpiece for Burman's politics.

Emerging onto the art scene in the early 1980s, Burman belongs to a generation of British artists of colour whose families had settled in postwar Britain. Her work was at its most political during this period, as she mirrored the social unrest and protest of the time and challenged society through her revolutionary art.

Chila Kumari Singh Burman
b.1957

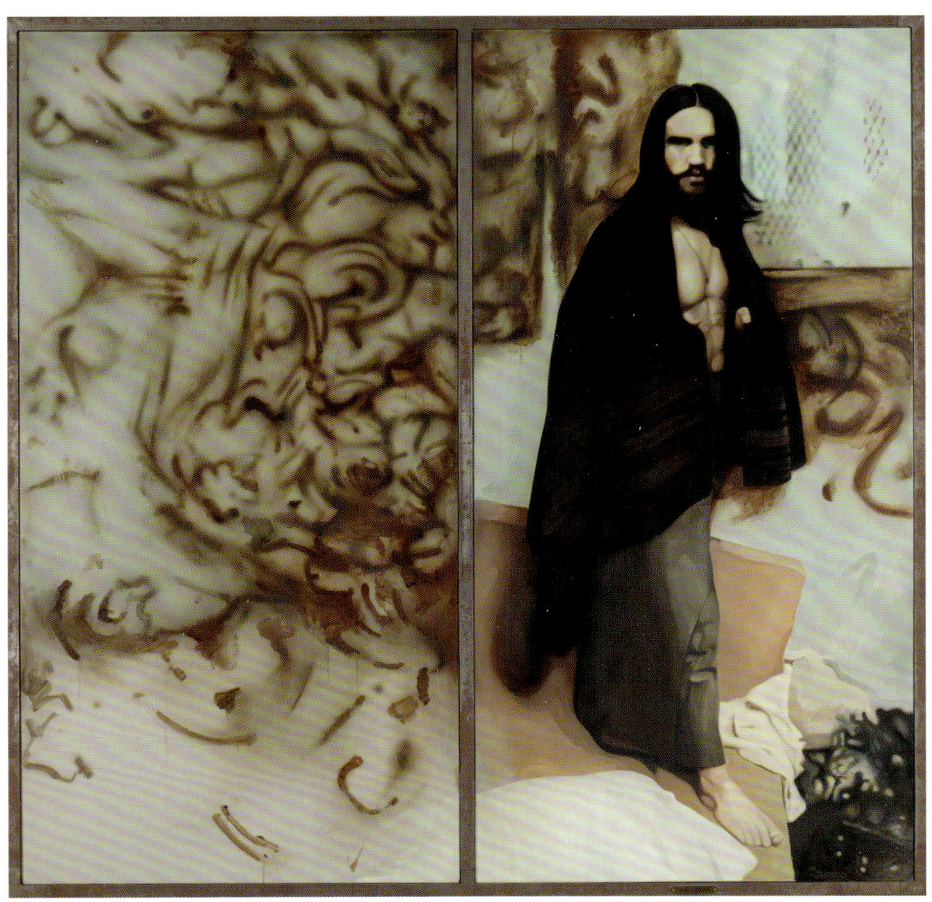

Pop art doesn't always bring forth associations with political commitment, but Richard Hamilton made politics his persistent concern. Hamilton was part of the Independent Group, a cohort of young artists, architects and critics emerging from the early 1950s, who made their analysis of contemporary life playful but cutting. By the time the Troubles in Northern Ireland were reaching peak crisis in the early 1980s, Hamilton was poised with the idea for *The citizen*, the first of three major works dedicated to the conflict. Evoking the tradition of history painting and grand altarpieces, instead of lapis lazuli Madonnas or gilded kings, we see a bedraggled, bearded young man, standing on a bare mattress with the murky detritus of slept-in sheets and wanton debris laying at his feet. Who is this 'citizen'? What about his stare is just so, well, troubling? As these questions spin, we begin to understand that we are looking at a prison cell, with the grated aperture behind the main character being the main clue. The man is Hugh Rooney, one of the lesser-known members of the IRA. The image finds its real-life source from a BBC documentary broadcast from the high-security prison near Belfast, known as the Maze, where IRA inmates were held. In 1976, the inmates demanded to be reinstated as political, not criminal, offenders, to attain better rights and living conditions. The British government refused. So, they stopped wearing their uniforms, cleaning themselves and grooming, then further protested by smearing excrement on the walls. A hunger strike followed, with Bobby Sands being the first to die, followed by nine others. Eighteen prison officers were also killed during the period of protests. Hamilton's recreation of this 'dirty protest' may present Rooney as a saint fallen from grace, but there is perilous revolt at the heart of this evocative scene.

Richard Hamilton
1922–2011

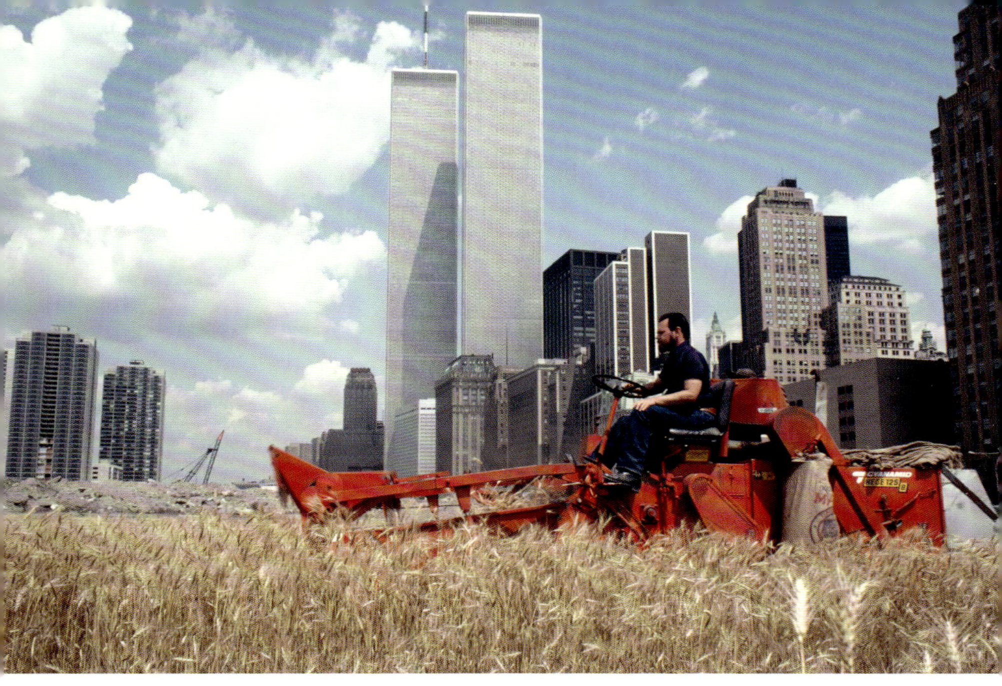

Wheatfield is an environmental piece by American Land artist Agnes Denes, which involved planting a 8,094-square-metre amber field of grain in a landfill in the shadow of the Twin Towers. Almost forty years later, it continues to be a supremely relevant work, the urgency of which is still rife. The site is awash with meaning; the landfill was created when the Twin Towers were built and is in close proximity to Wall Street, home of the stock exchange and where wheat is traded – a shiny beacon of commodification. The landfill was full of infertile rubble and waste, so Denes cleared it away and shipped in enough fresh soil to substantially cover the site and, with a few volunteers, dug 285 furrows to plant North Dakotan wheat by hand. The 450 kg of wheat that was harvested then travelled in the touring exhibition *International Art Show for the End of World Hunger*, which ran from 1987 to 1990 and travelled to twenty-eight cities, and where visitors were given packets of seed, which they then planted in solidarity with her project.

Wheat, at the hands of Denes, is a powerful symbol; it is food, grown from the earth – it connects us all. Denes's public intervention highlights our misplaced priorities and deteriorating human values, and in a place where the powers that be couldn't ignore. At the foot of the World Trade Center, facing the Statue of Liberty, it is both critical and hopeful. Denes's lasting message is, if we want change, we must dig deep.

Agnes Denes
b.1931

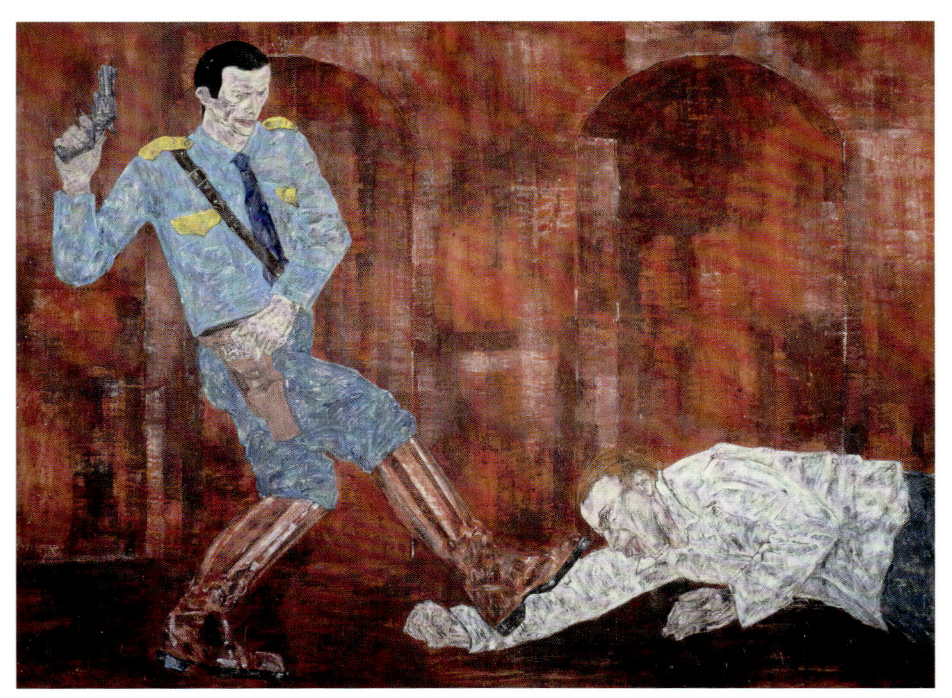

American painter Leon Golub dedicated his almost sixty-year career to exploring the trauma of social violence through his art. In *White Squad V*, part of a seven-painting series inspired by real events in Central America, Golub immortalises a harrowing scene at a monumental scale. The series focuses on the Salvadoran death squads, a right-wing military force responsible for countless deaths during the Salvadoran Civil War, and, in this moment, which shows a heavy-booted policeman stepping on the outstretched arm of a person sprawled on the ground, rendered on an unstretched three by four-metre canvas, his barbaric realism is at its most visceral. At such a gargantuan scale, the viewer almost falls into the anguish, which is made all the more affecting by the painting's size, coming face to face with a scene unsettlingly current in light of the ongoing cries for the demilitarisation and restructuring of the police. Golub's technique is appropriately abrasive: layer after layer of acrylic paint is dissolved with poured solvent then scraped away with a meat cleaver. Ever elemental, the ghostly images confront you with the stark reality of power and torture on the fringes of Western politics in Central America. The canvases have received such a handling by Golub that their dense flat surfaces reveal exposed fibres – like the wounding of skin or blistering of flesh – thereby becoming expressions of violence in a more literal sense. Golub attached himself to events that warped culture, directing his critique initially to the Vietnam War while he was living and working with his wife, the artist Nancy Spero, in Paris for five years before devoting his attention to other conflicts. Golub monumentalises terror, dwarfing the viewer to its power so we can understand just how quickly it can inflate and get out of control.

Leon Golub
1922–2004

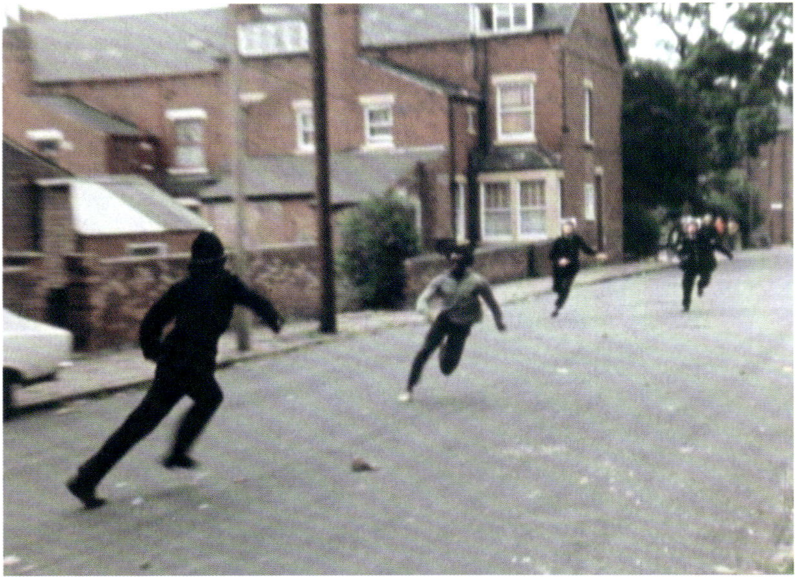

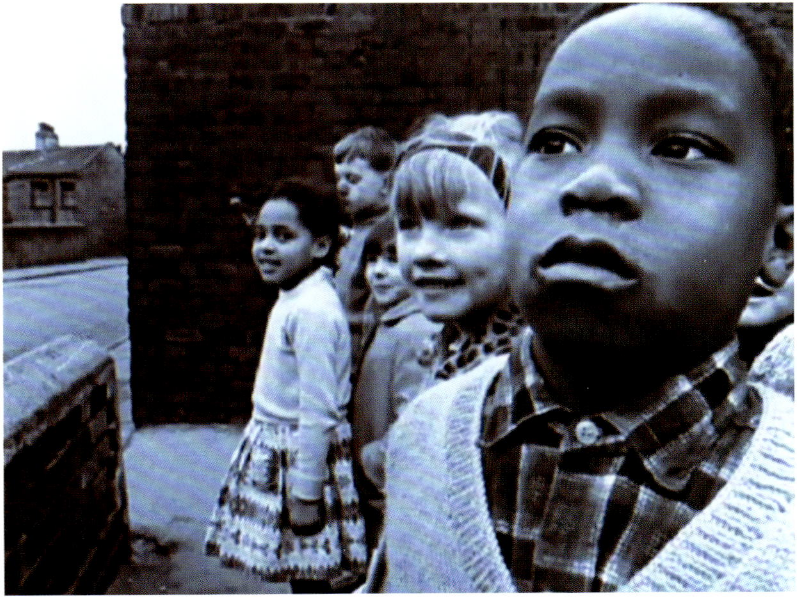

*Handsworth
Songs* 1986
Film; single-
channel, 16 mm,
colour and sound
58 min 33 sec

At the heart of protest is education and the revelation and liberation of the truth, and so documentary is a powerful rallying medium. *Handsworth Songs* takes its title from the riots of Handsworth, Birmingham, UK, which erupted during September 1985. The densely layered documentary embodies the hopes and dreams of Black British people, postwar and in the wake of the frequent civil disturbances in the 1980s. The London-based Black Audio Film Collective, a group of sociology, psychology and fine art students, consisting of (at the time) John Akomfrah (who directed *Handsworth Songs*), Reece Auguiste, Eddie George, Lina Gopaul, Avril Johnson, Trevor Mathison and David Lawson, made the film in 1986. This relatively new fashion of dialogue overlaid on film images engages the viewer with topics of Britain's colonial past, public and private memories and the struggles of race and class. The complex multi-layered narratives defy linear, chronological and, therefore, conventional readings and reject the idea of a singular, homogeneous Black 'voice'. It is uncomfortable viewing; an affront in many ways as, frame after frame, images, spectacles and questions shift our perceptions and subtly bend our attachments to meaning. No two viewings are the same; sit back and be changed.

Black Audio Film Collective

WHEN RACISM & SEXISM ARE NO LONGER FASHIONABLE, WHAT WILL YOUR ART COLLECTION BE WORTH?

The art market won't bestow mega-buck prices on the work of a few white males forever. For the 17.7 million you just spent on a single Jasper Johns painting, you could have bought at least one work by all of these women and artists of color:

Bernice Abbott
Anni Albers
Sofonisba Anguisolla
Diane Arbus
Vanessa Bell
Isabel Bishop
Rosa Bonheur
Elizabeth Bougereau
Margaret Bourke-White
Romaine Brooks
Julia Margaret Cameron
Emily Carr
Rosalba Carriera
Mary Cassatt
Constance Marie Charpentier
Imogen Cunningham
Sonia Delaunay

Elaine de Kooning
Lavinia Fontana
Meta Warwick Fuller
Artemisia Gentileschi
Marguérite Gérard
Natalia Goncharova
Kate Greenaway
Barbara Hepworth
Eva Hesse
Hannah Hoch
Anna Huntingdon
May Howard Jackson
Frida Kahlo
Angelica Kauffmann
Hilma af Klimt
Kathe Kollwitz
Lee Krasner

Dorothea Lange
Marie Laurencin
Edmonia Lewis
Judith Leyster
Barbara Longhi
Dora Maar
Lee Miller
Lisette Model
Paula Modersohn-Becker
Tina Modotti
Berthe Morisot
Grandma Moses
Gabriele Münter
Alice Neel
Louise Nevelson
Georgia O'Keeffe
Meret Oppenheim

Sarah Peale
Ljubova Popova
Olga Rosanova
Nellie Mae Rowe
Rachel Ruysch
Kay Sage
Augusta Savage
Vavara Stepanova
Florine Stettheimer
Sophie Taeuber-Arp
Alma Thomas
Marietta Robusti Tintoretto
Suzanne Valadon
Remedios Varo
Elizabeth Vigée Le Brun
Laura Wheeling Waring

Information courtesy of Christie's, Sotheby's, Mayer's International Auction Records and Leonard's Annual Price Index of Auctions.

Please send $ and comments to:
Box 1056 Cooper Sta. NY, NY 10276 **GUERRILLA GIRLS** CONSCIENCE OF THE ART WORLD

Masked with gorilla heads, the Guerrilla Girls have been punking art-world sexism and racism since 1985. *Guerrilla Girls Talk Back* is a series of posters from the group of anonymous American women artists who set out to shake up the art world. Protecting their identities in public by wearing gorilla masks and going under the pseudonyms of deceased female figures of renown, such as Gertrude Stein and Frida Kahlo, they make it their *modus operandi* to expose the sexual and racial discrimination rife in the art world. As the self-dubbed 'conscience of the art world', the brazen bunch started a poster campaign targeted at museums, dealers, curators, artists and others who they felt were responsible for or complicit in the exclusion of women and non-white artists from the art sphere. Adopting the style of advertising and flyposting – an accessible and democratic way of pushing their battle cries – the cohort first plastered these posters in the streets of New York's SoHo at the dead of night, and then within the city's museums. At one point, you could purchase a book from the Guggenheim bookshop and turn the pages to a bright, neon flyer posing the question 'WHEN RACISM & SEXISM ARE NO LONGER FASHIONABLE, WHAT WILL YOUR ART COLLECTION BE WORTH?', then step outside the museum and see a bus roll past with an advertisement asking 'Do women have to be naked to get into the Met. Museum?' The Guerrilla Girls wanted to be heard. Armed with a toolkit of wit, irony and bolshiness, they put a critical middle finger up to double standards.

Guerrilla Girls
formed 1985

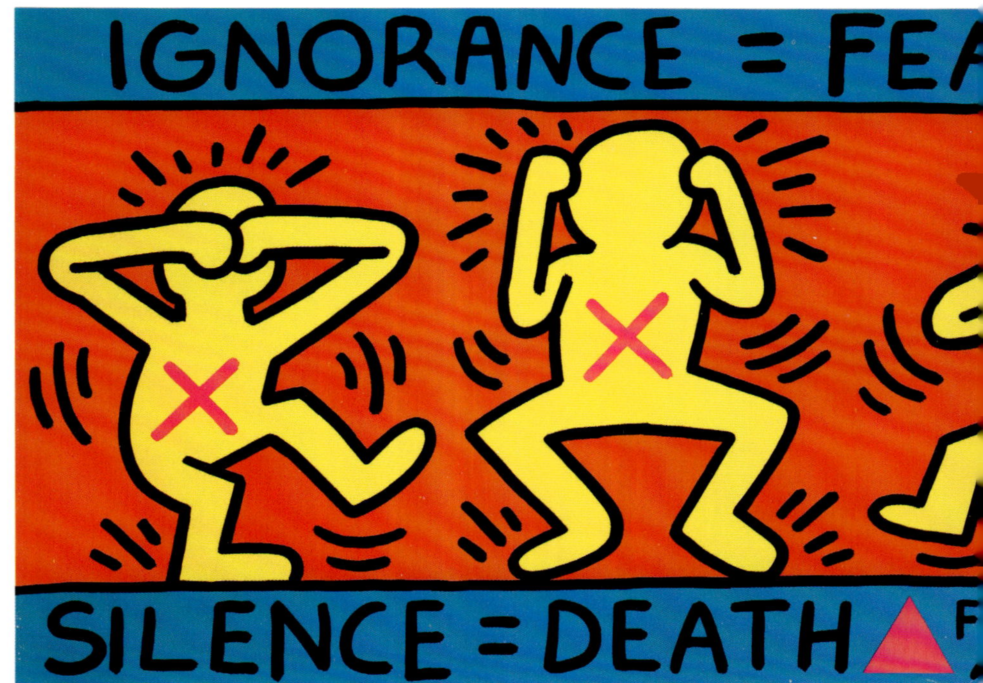

Ignorance = Fear / Silence = Death 1989 Offset lithograph on paper 61.1 × 109.4

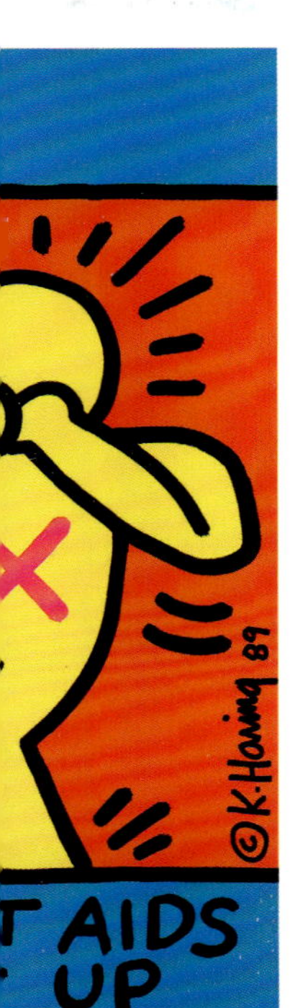

Bright, bold, primary colours, cartoon-like figures and a sobering message – political activism punctuates Keith Haring's artistic oeuvre. The artist made posters, marched for nuclear disarmament, rallied against apartheid and confronted religious oppression in his seemingly bright and bubbly cartoons. As the AIDS crisis took hold of the world, Haring honed his focus in his final years.

The iconic *Ignorance = Fear / Silence = Death* 1989 poster is bolshy and to the point: a memorable slogan with piercingly direct symbolic resonance. The three figures cover their eyes, ears and mouths, perhaps referencing the Japanese pictorial maxim of the three wise monkeys, who embody the proverbial phrase 'see no evil, hear no evil, speak no evil', and also the idea of turning a blind eye, therefore highlighting Haring's pressing message.

The stakes were high – in the beginnings of the AIDS epidemic, the government and mainstream media famously ignored the crisis. So Haring reached into his artistic toolbox and fashioned something with a direct impact. The poster he created is a simplification of one of his paintings from the same year, *Silence = Death*. The pink triangle at the bottom is an inversion of an emblem for gay men, devised by the artist-activist collective Gran Fury. Unlike a manifesto, *Ignorance = Fear / Silence = Death* is not wordy and doesn't require time to read or digest. Simple, attention-grabbing, it hits you in the core; Haring warns us that if we put our heads in the sand for too long, we may just wake up to a ruined world.

Keith Haring
1958–90

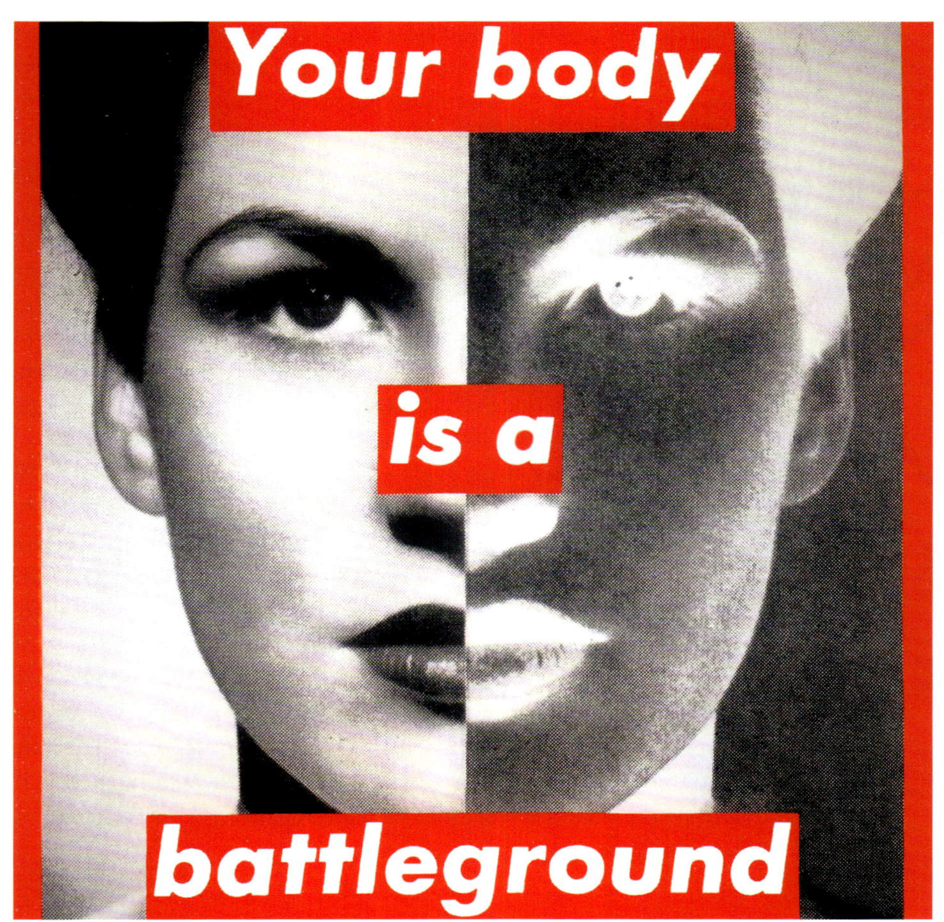

Your body
is a
battleground

*Untitled
(Your body is
a battleground)*
1989
Photographic
screenprint
on vinyl 284.48
× 284.48

Barbara Kruger's media-based works force us into feeling. Politics is her native tongue and her evisceration of cultural hierarchies harnesses her ideologies. She makes us question our inherent consumer desires and the violence of the male gaze.

Untitled (Your body is a battleground) is her timeless and iconic declaration which, like much of her work, employs tabloid-like language and the aesthetics of popular media to mock propaganda by turning it into protest. Her work is instantly recognisable: phrases range from the fiercely political to acidic criticisms of culture to destabilising existentialism, delivered through the visual aesthetics of advertising and slogans. Kruger began her career as a graphic designer for magazines, and so her visual language of collage and investigations of American culture through lenses of consumerism, power and gender is not surprising.

In 1989, the year in which this work was made, protestors in the US rallied against a new wave of anti-abortion laws that were slowly unravelling the Supreme Court ruling that upheld the constitutional right to have an abortion. Why are the reproductive rights of women an open debate? Why has the female form been over-policed but, ironically, under-protected? Kruger knew why, and she used her art to fight against the patriarchy. *Untitled (Your body is a battleground)* began as her protest flyer for the Women's March on Washington, since she vehemently supported reproductive freedom, though its battle cry has come to represent all matters of injustices against women. The woman's face, stark and unflinchingly resolute, is bisected into positive and negative exposures, emblazoned with text, implicating the viewer via the use of 'your'. Plain and profound, this is art as dissent: a powerful tool to rally support and encourage us to speak out. Even in the #MeToo era, women's rights and bodily autonomy are under constant threat. This work is just as prescient and persuasive now, over thirty years later, as it was then.

Barbara Kruger
b.1945

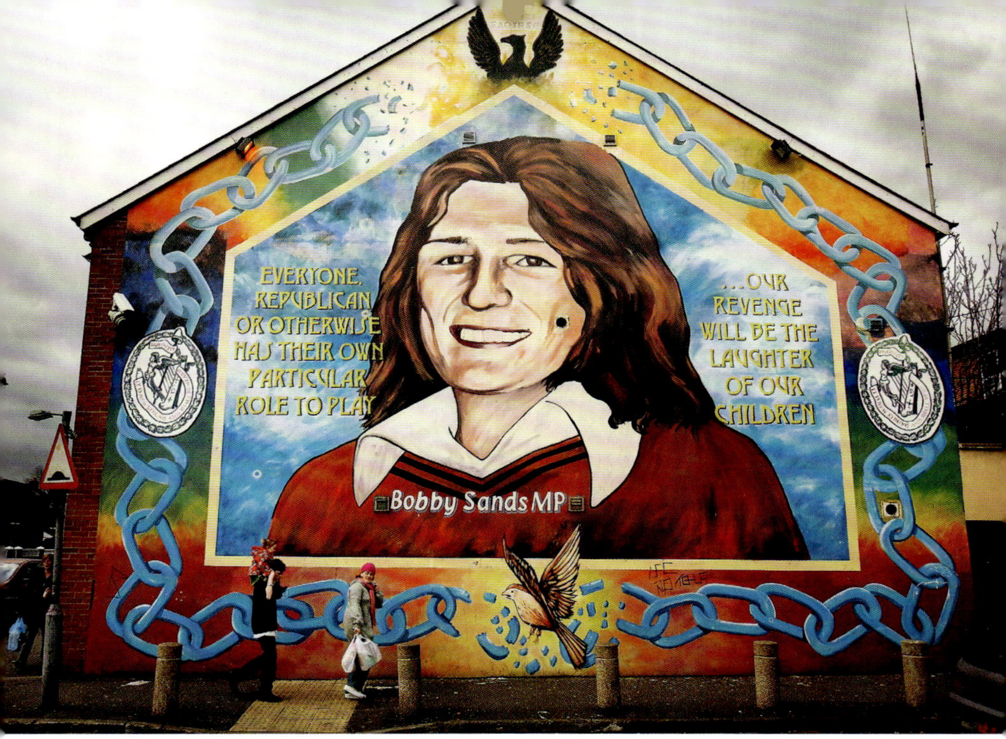

EVERYONE, REPUBLICAN OR OTHERWISE HAS THEIR OWN PARTICULAR ROLE TO PLAY
...OUR REVENGE WILL BE THE LAUGHTER OF OUR CHILDREN
Bobby Sands MP

Northern Ireland has a troubled political past; only a few decades ago Belfast was a city at war. The Belfast murals memorialise the unrest between nationalist and unionist citizens over the partition of Northern Ireland in 1921 under British rule, with violence continuing to erupt from that time well into the 1980s between those who wished to reunite and those who preferred to remain separate. As the conflicts unfolded, paramilitary groups – the nationalist Republicans and the unionist Loyalists – emerged, filling the streets with violence and inspiring almost 2,000 wall paintings in their wake. In these murals, key figures during the Troubles are memorialised, for example in paintings dedicated to Bobby Sands, a member of the Irish Republican Army (IRA) and UK Parliament. He led the 1981 hunger strike and died while in HM Prison Maze. Another mural, 'Can it Change? We Believe!', erected by unionists, depicts a family evacuated from their home by Republican paramilitary groups, flanked by two news scrolls from the *Belfast Telegraph*. The right-hand scroll is poignantly empty, save for a large question mark, symbolising the unknown future of Northern Ireland. The proliferation of the murals gets to the very core of protest – grassroots and in the language of the people, they are both protest and propaganda, used by opposing sides to fight for what they believe in and rally for others to join them. Murals have an ephemeral quality and an enduring power. They are a critical intervention into urban and domestic space. Even though the protests have quietened, the collective voices of these protestors can still be heard and seen on the streets of Belfast.

Various artists

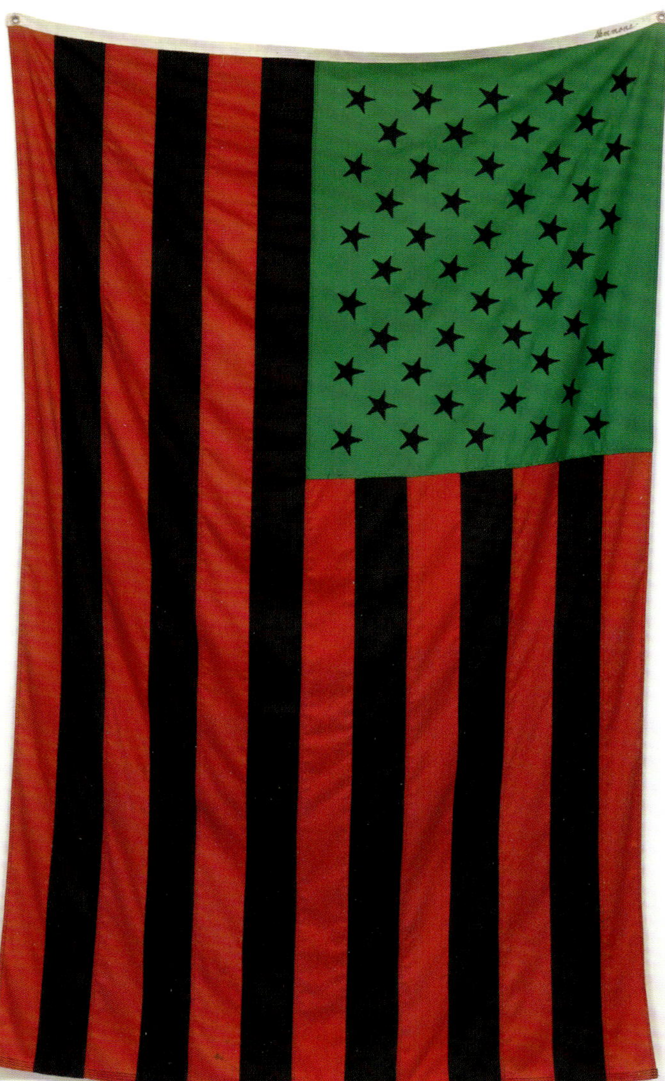

African American Flag 1990
Canvas and grommets
240 × 149.9

African American Flag, one of David Hammons's most iconic works, is a subversive subsumption of the US flag into the colours of the Pan African flag. In keeping with Hammons's enthusiasm for transforming politically charged found objects and refashioning them to form intricate allegories, the work was conceived for the watershed *Black USA* exhibition in 1990 at the Museum Overholland, Amsterdam. Disrupting the idealistic associations of the American Dream with its messages and ideas of inclusion, Hammons is representing 'Black America'; a narrative historically left out. With echoes of the Duchampian readymade and the raw viscerality of outsider art, Hammons disarms the symbol of the American flag. He imbues it with further meaning – expanding, not reducing, the content and presenting a sharp socio-political commentary relating to themes of representation, race, injustice and visibility in equal measure. The Pan African flag, from which Hammons draws the colourway, was designed by the activist Marcus Garvey to represent the African diaspora: the red and black signify shared blood and skin colour, while the green alludes to Africa's natural lushness. The flag was adopted by the Universal Negro Improvement Association and African Communities League in 1920 and gained popularity during the 1960s Black Power movement. Hammons's visual and linguistic transformation leaves the work's message open-ended, and maintains its enduring relevance. There is an optimism to the work, as well as truth: hopeful and honest, Hammons reminds us to question what we see and believe.

David Hammons
b.1943

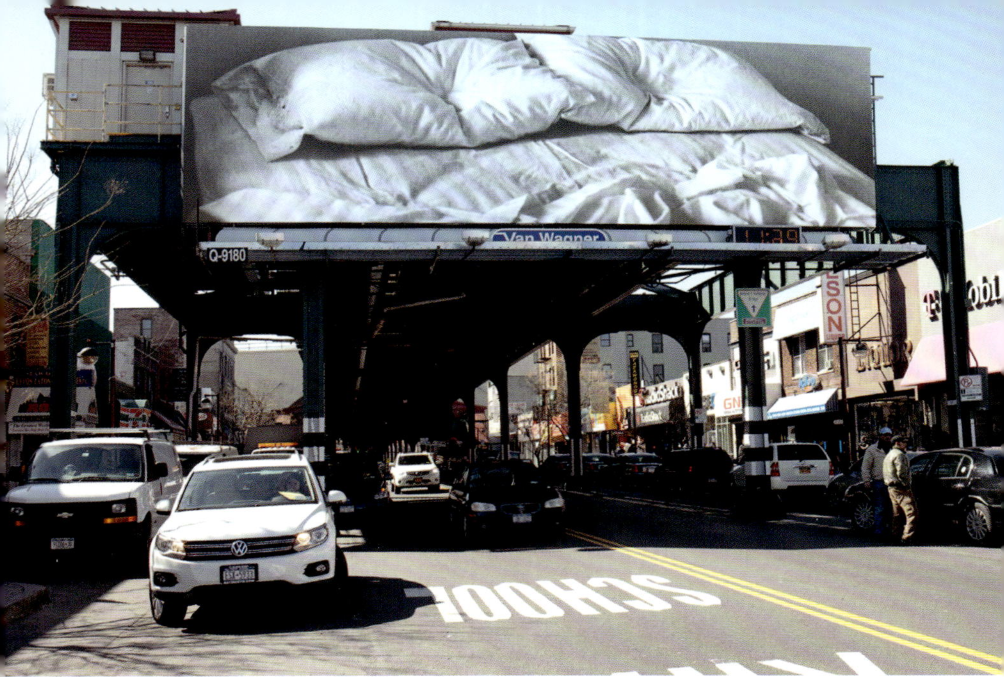
Van Wagner
Q-9180
SCHOOL

Felix Gonzalez-Torres made unmade beds political. *"Untitled"* is a stark, black-and-white image of the rumpled sheets and pillows of the artist's bed that makes us see such sites – usually places of sexuality, comfort and rest – in unexpected ways. The work was first exhibited in 1992 in twenty-four outdoor billboard locations throughout New York City (in Manhattan and the surrounding Burroughs), and one indoor location. The image reproduced here is from a later iteration that comprised of six billboards in outdoor locations throughout New York City, and one indoor location, as part of the exhibition *Print/Out*, at the Museum of Modern Art, New York, in 2012. The work collided the contrasting worlds of the public and private. The collective absence of bodies, signified by the depression in the middle of each pillow, became a memorialisation of loss amid the AIDS crisis. With the formation of AIDS Coalition to Unleash Power (ACTUP) in 1987, questions about the relationship between art and politics, took on new significance for gay artists. Gonzalez-Torres's protest as elegy is testament to a seldom apparent representation of homosexuality that resonated particularly at a time when the US President, Ronald Reagan, notoriously didn't use the word 'AIDS' until 12,000 people had already died from the disease. Gonzalez-Torres's wrinkled sheets and head-shaped grooves in pillows then became a protest for the recognition of same-sex love. Abstract, subtle and poignant, *"Untitled"*, like much of the artist's work, uses the language of the everyday to open our eyes to the present and stand for change.

Felix Gonzalez-Torres
1957–96

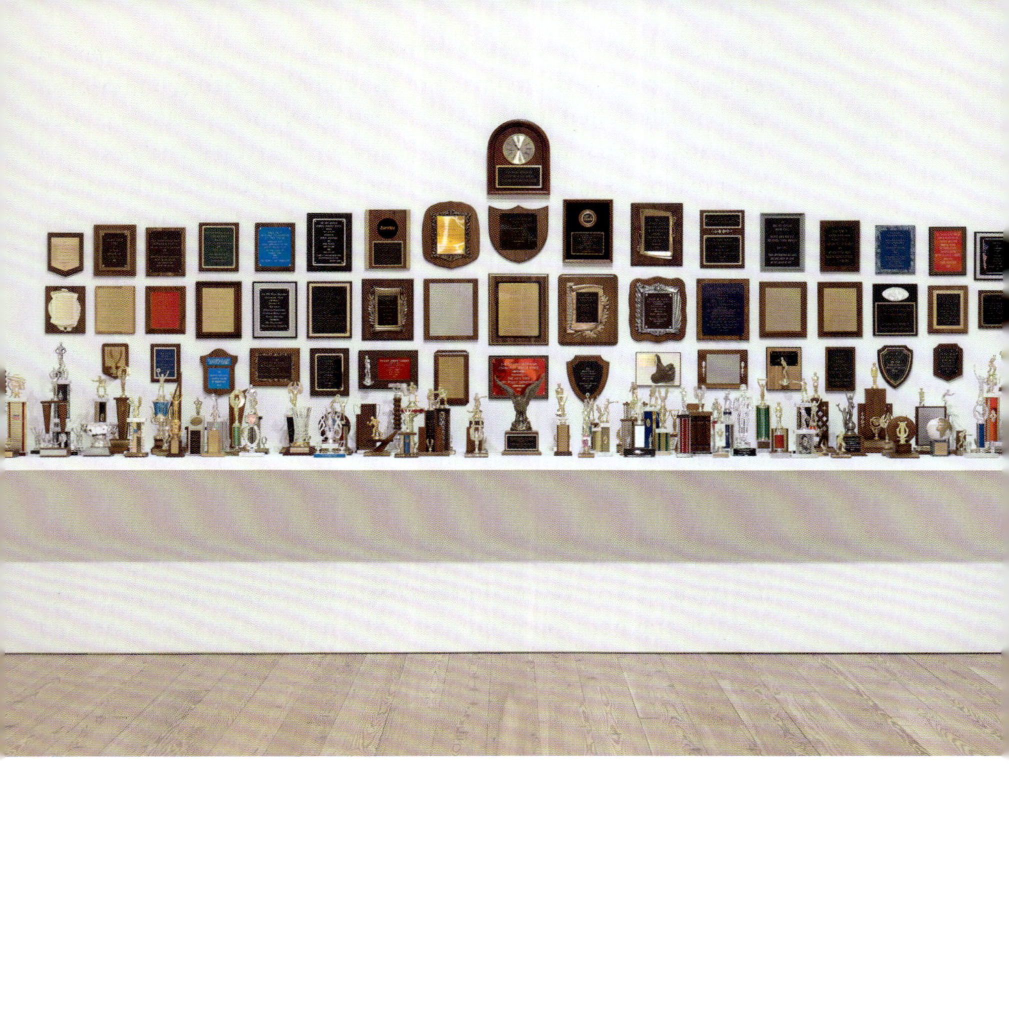

*Some of the
Greatest Hits
of the New York
City Police
Department:
A Celebration
of Meritorious
Achievement in
the Community
1994, Engraved
trophies,
Dimensions
variable*

How can trophies be protests? This powerful installation consists of rows of trophies, awards and plaques – glittering symbols of achievements and excellence, and strongly associated with sports, athletics and general superiority. The title of Pope's work gives some clues as to its political agenda: the artist wants us to rub our eyes and look beyond the shiny glitz and the generic figures these objects depict. For those are police officers atop the trophies; police officers holding guns. Below, engraved is not 'Basketball Player of the Year' but the real names of officers and the dates when they were recognised for a particular service. After this initial disruption, the realisation hits the viewer that they are in fact witnessing the negation of police brutality in America, imprinted on a laudatory display of excellence. The project was catalysed by the death of Leonard Barnett in 1977, after which Pope discovered these twisted awards – one example being the officer who received a pay rise after killing Eric Garner in 2014. In the wake of the death of George Floyd in 2020, and the subsequent protests and conviction of the police officer responsible, Derek Chauvin, the call for police reform and the rise of the Black Lives Matter movement, this work is ever poignant as a call to arms. Pope is saying 'no more'.

Carl Pope
b.1961

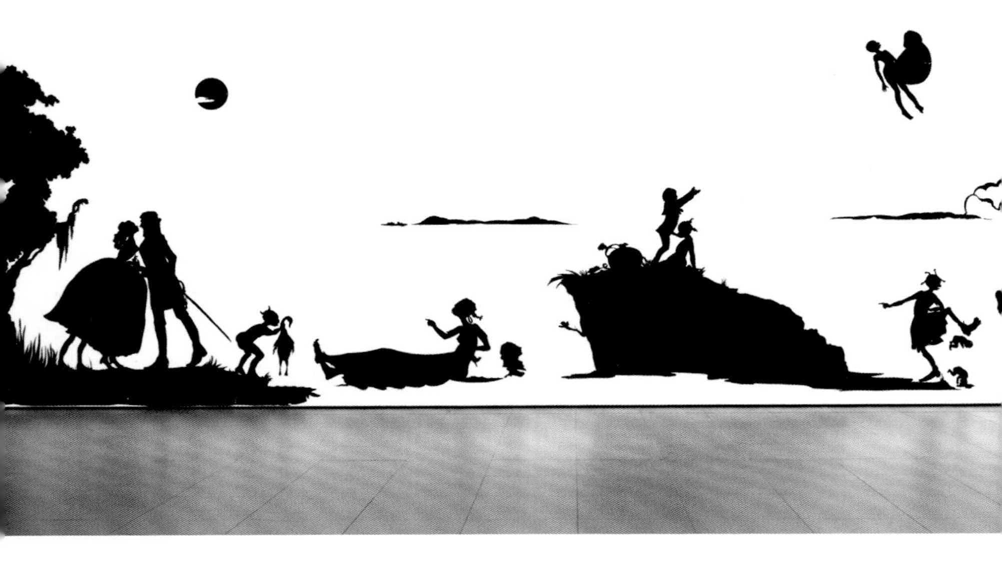

*Gone: An
Historical
Romance of a
Civil War as It
Occurred b'tween
the Dusky Thighs
of One Young
Negress and
Her Heart* 1994
Cut paper on
wall c.396.2
× 1524

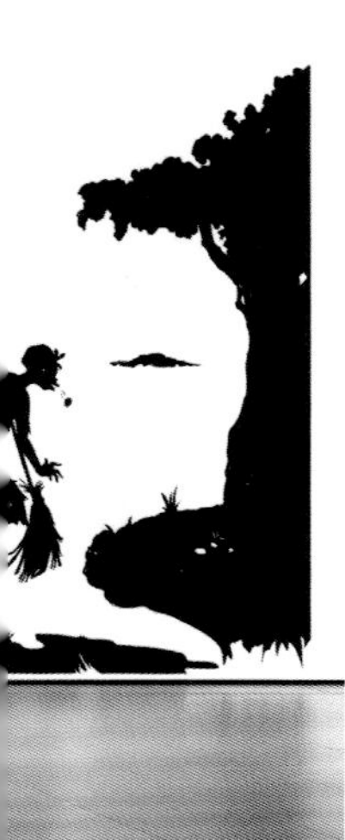

Kara Walker's now iconic shadow paintings ask us to deal with some of the most insidious parts of our history. In the work here, we see the genesis of the artist's signature style and expression: black cut-out silhouettes, caricaturing Antebellum figures starkly against crisp white walls, often with violent and sexual scenarios, and a twist of an uncanny, dark humour mixed in. An evolution of the history painting, here Walker is giving voice and image to histories that have been concealed or buried. Decidedly Victorian in style, Walker resuscitates the eighteenth-century cut-out paper technique, while also referencing shadow puppets and the ideas of lost cultures, 'shadows', to critique historical narratives of slavery and the subsequent proliferation of ethnic stereotyping. The work directly references *Gone With the Wind*, the 1936 American Civil War novel by Margaret Mitchell, which, together with the subsequent 1939 film – still the highest-grossing film of all time – was important, perhaps unintentional, propaganda, that shaped the popular understanding of the war. The book is a fitting representation of prejudice, and after the film rights were sold, there were many objections from African Americans, who feared the film would incite violence, spread bigotry and derail a proposed federal anti-lynching bill. After its release, there were protests outside cinemas in Chicago, Washington and other cities. In her narrative, Walker asks us to question what we read while also calling for a more authentic viewing of Black history. Her monumental tale sees enslaved people on leashes, fellatio, a man floating with an extremely swollen penis and a woman giving birth with abandon as her new-born child drops to the ground. Depicting the havoc that we have come to hear through stories of slavery and the Antebellum South, the artist questions how much is true, and how much served as a means to perpetuate a narrative of savagery. Walker is protesting stereotypes and critiquing history in one swoop, which are as grotesque and surreal as humanity itself.

Kara Walker
b.1969

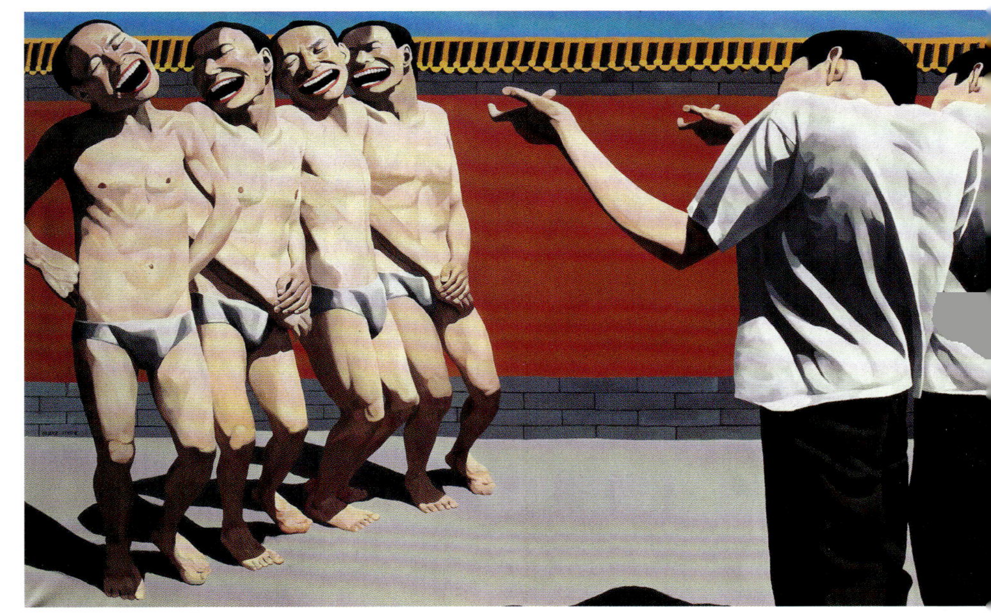

Execution
1995
Oil paint
on canvas
150 × 300

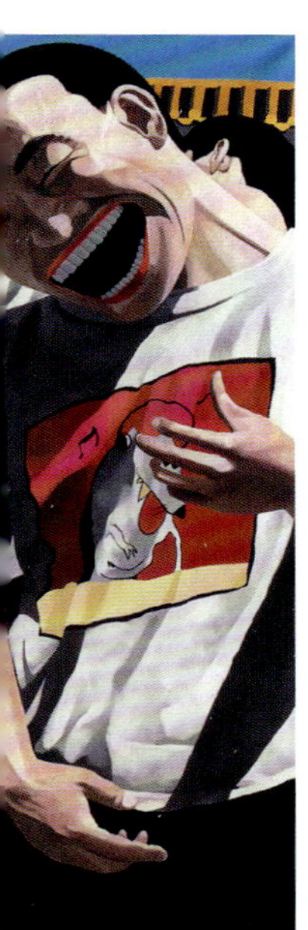

Execution is one of Yue Minjun's most politically rousing works. His trademark grinning clones gather in two groups; one set laughing in white underwear, and the other wielding invisible guns, as one member turns towards and laughs in the face of the viewer. It is unquestionably a mockery of human conflict. Drawing on references to *The 3rd of May 1808: The Execution of the Defenders of Madrid* 1814 by Francisco de Goya (1746–1828) and *The Execution of the Emperor Maximilian of Mexico* 1867–9 by Édouard Manet (1832–83) the painting's mock execution fuses cynical realism with political critique. Set against the red wall of the Imperial Palace, the painting clearly references the 1989 Tiananmen Square massacre when hundreds, if not thousands, of Chinese protestors lost their lives in clashes with the military. The protests were a demonstration for democracy: under the leadership of Deng Xiaoping, citizens believed their independence, freedom of speech and freedom of the press were being restricted. The protests began on 15 April and ended on 4 June 1989, when the Chinese government declared martial law, which triggered immeasurable violence and saw troops equipped with assault rifles and tanks, leading to further suppression of Chinese citizens' civil rights. The artist, in 2011, explained on CNN: 'I want the audience not to think of one thing or one place or one event. The whole world's the background. As I said, the viewer should not link this painting to Tiananmen. But Tiananmen is the catalyst for conceiving of this painting.'

The figures to the left of *Execution* have their hands by their sides, notably not up in resistance as in Goya's painting, and the other group hold imaginary guns. They don't fear death, and join in the laughs with the opposition. A sense of fear and disturbing unknown pervades this image. Laughter can counteract helplessness; it is a coping mechanism and unveils some absurd aspects of the human condition – but can it be a sort of resistance?

Yue Minjun
b.1962

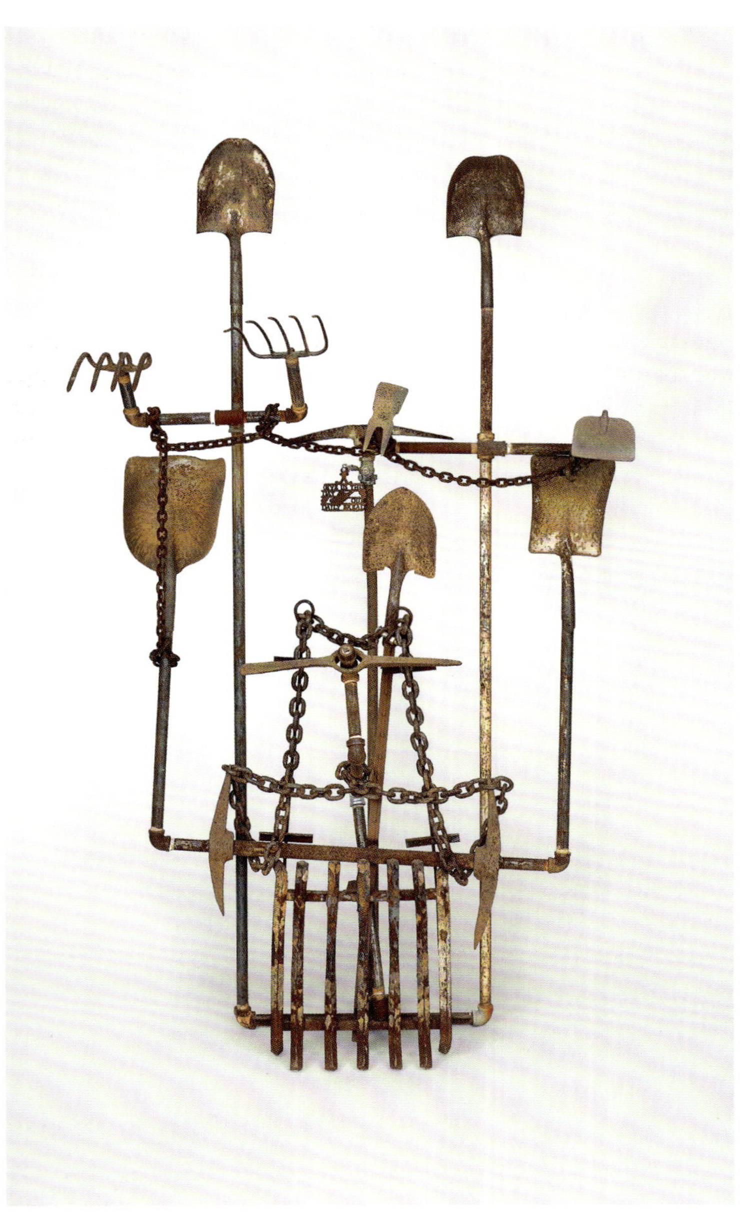

Four Hundred Years of Free Labor 1995 Welded found metal 266.7 × 152.4 × 137.2

In this work, Joe Minter tells of the 400-hundred-year story of Africans in America; how Africans were captured and enslaved. Composed of old, rusty metal tools – pitchforks, pickaxe heads, a hoe and shovels – and bound by chains, the upright-standing materials look like a human form. Jarring and menacing, the confrontational work evokes the forced labour to which African Americans were subjected, from harvesting cotton to the chain gangs of the twentieth century. The pitchforks seem to reach out and claw at you, while the spade heads stare blankly in disbelief, perhaps pondering the years of complacency in the face of injustice. Minter's assemblage of tools is a homage to the anonymous labourers who once wielded them, now put together to confront, and critique, their past oppression. Works such as this this one stand in the 'African Village in America', part of Minter's property in Birmingham, Alabama.

Joe Minter
b.1943

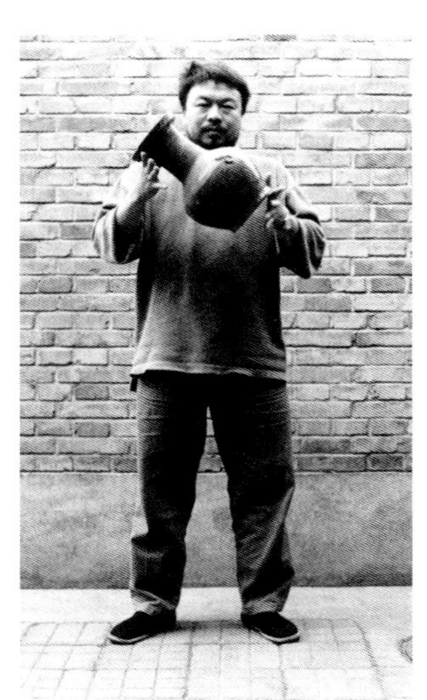 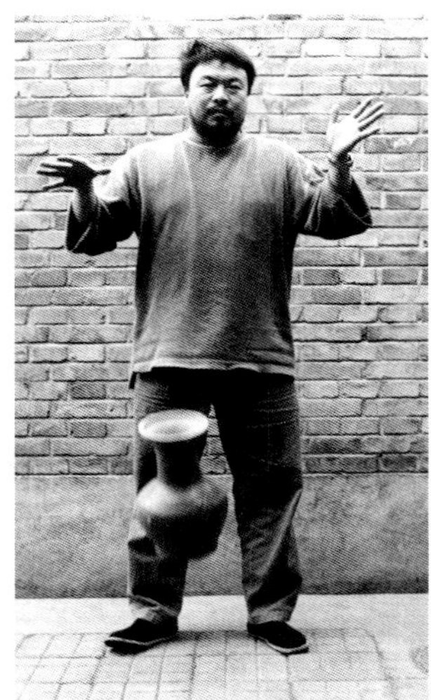 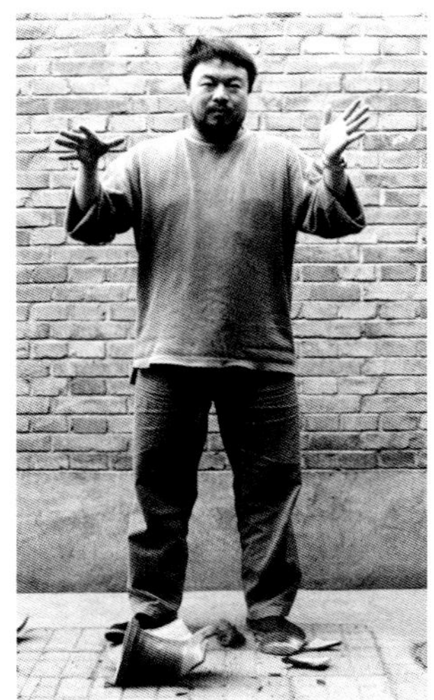

Activist artist Ai Weiwei does not shy away from controversy. One of his most iconic artworks, his 'cultural readymade', is a photograph of him dropping a 2,000-year-old ceremonial urn in three stages: grasped in his hand, floating in mid-air, then crashing at his feet. The artefact, of considerable value and symbolic cultural worth, originates from the Han Dynasty (206 BCE–220 CE), a defining period in the history of Chinese civilisation. Deliberately destroying an important representation of that history is a shocking demonstration and urges us to question how and who creates cultural value and distils it into objects.

Ai Weiwei also sought to point out the damages of General Mao's regime: the destruction of the object was a crystal-clear assimilation of how the Communist regime impacted the 'elite'. Countering outrage, the artist retold a statement from Mao – 'The only way of building a new world is by destroying the old one' – a reference to the destruction of antiquities throughout China's Cultural Revolution (1966–76), and the conception that in order to create a new society one must destroy the *sì jiù* (the Four Olds: old customs, habits, culture and ideas). By dropping the urn, Ai Weiwei urged for the penny also to drop – and revolted against the governance of China, questioning how it should be built anew. He then went on to dip 2,000-year-old vases in paint and impress them with Coca-Cola logos: he wants us to look to the past, take it apart and fashion a new future.

Ai Weiwei
b.1957

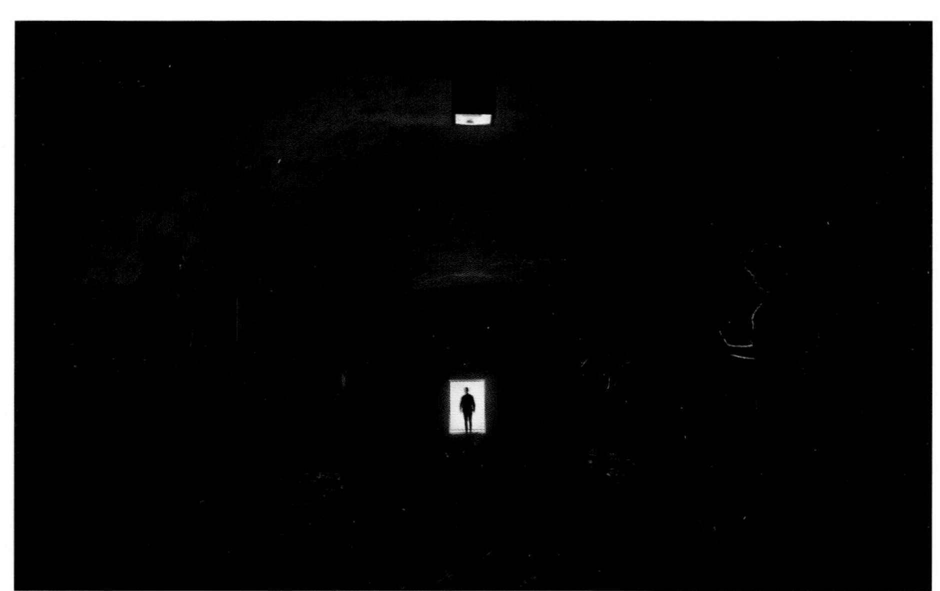

Untitled (Havana 2000) 2000
Sugar cane bagasse, video (black and white, silent; 4 min 37 sec), and live performance. Installation: 5000 × 1200 × 400

Tania Bruguera was born in Havana, Cuba, and bore witness to what she perceived as the failings of the Cuban Revolution – economic hardship, creative censorship and unregulated power. *Untitled (Havana 2000)* debuted at the 7th Havana Biennial and is undoubtedly one of her most polemic works. The installation was first shown in a military vault in La Cabaña, a fortress where Cuban counter-revolutionaries were imprisoned, tortured and killed. The artwork is as chilling as the site's history, and as viewers entered the space they were confronted with seemingly endless darkness and floors lined with milled sugar cane, Cuba's most lucrative export. Treading cautiously into the dark abyss they encounter nude male performers feverishly scratching themselves as a video of Fidel Castro plays on a small television. There are strange power dynamics at play here: we are forced to reckon with both the visible and more private psychological manifestations of governmental oppression. Castro is curiously vulnerable, as he removes his military uniform and reveals he is not wearing a bulletproof vest – or is that cocky assurance in his smile and is he showing off his indomitability? Bruguera demonstrates the bravado that military-grade protection afforded Castro. Artists were specifically forbidden from criticising his regime; not that that bothered Bruguera. She initially omitted the Castro film from her proposal, and from the opening day. Once the exhibition organisers discovered the addition of the film, they shut off the electricity around the vault, immersing the entire space in darkness. Once the lights came back on, Bruguera's art was censored – the video was not allowed to play. But her point had been made. Performance and participation continue to punctuate Bruguera's activist art. She brings the lived experience of oppressed communities into the art space and into a democratised society for us to reckon with.

Tania Bruguera
b.1968

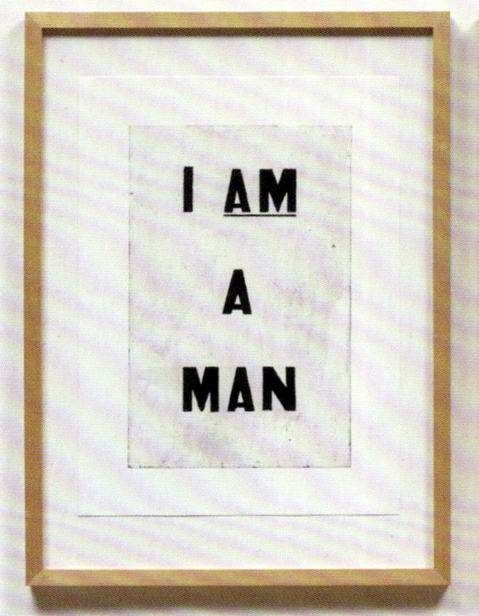

I AM
A
MAN

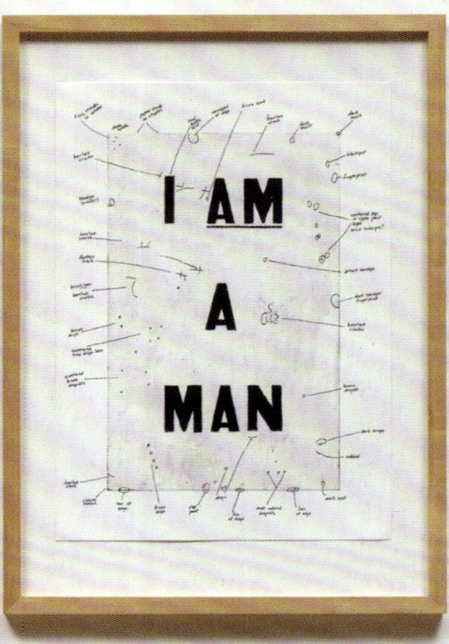

I AM
A
MAN

Condition Report 2000
Screenprint in
two parts 81.1
× 57.6 each

The words I AM A MAN is a rallying cry that calls to human compassion. Ralph Ellison, in the prologue to his novel *Invisible Man* 1952, states 'I am an invisible man.' Both statements are reclamations of and protests for visibility. They are a call to action, and a demand to be seen and understood. The statement I AM A MAN was the central component of a 1988 painting by Ligon, *Untitled (I Am a Man)*, though it is so much more than four words, bold, black set against white. It is fraught with history. The painting is undoubtedly one of Glenn Ligon's most iconic works, as an artist best known for employing text and language to tell narratives of American history particularly relating to slavery and civil rights. *Untitled (I Am a Man)* also references the civil rights protest placard that was carried in Memphis, Tennessee, in 1968 by striking African American sanitation workers revolting against the wrongful deaths of co-workers from faulty equipment, low wages and unsafe working conditions, and was subsequently taken up at the Martin Luther King memorial march after the activist's assassination that same year.

The surface of Ligon's painting is rough; it is tired and weathered. It s as if the work has borne the brunt of the daily micro and macro aggressions profuse in the African American experience. This theme is also explored in *Condition Report*, illustrated here, a diptych comprising two prints of the 1988 painting, with the right panel including annotations by the conservator Michael Duffy. The analysis of and writing on this work is political. The scars and struggles are indexed; every smudge, fingerprint and manhandling recorded. The way the work endures procedural analysis draws clear links to the degradation of the subject matter, the Black male. The material components are scrutinised and penalised; much like those the artist and this artwork seek to stand up for.

Glenn Ligon
b.1960

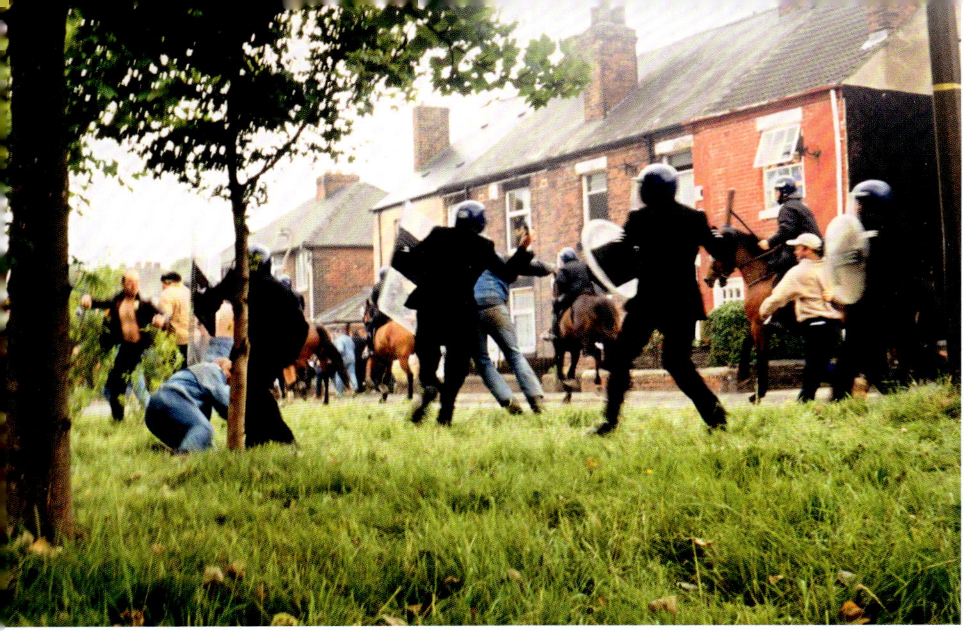

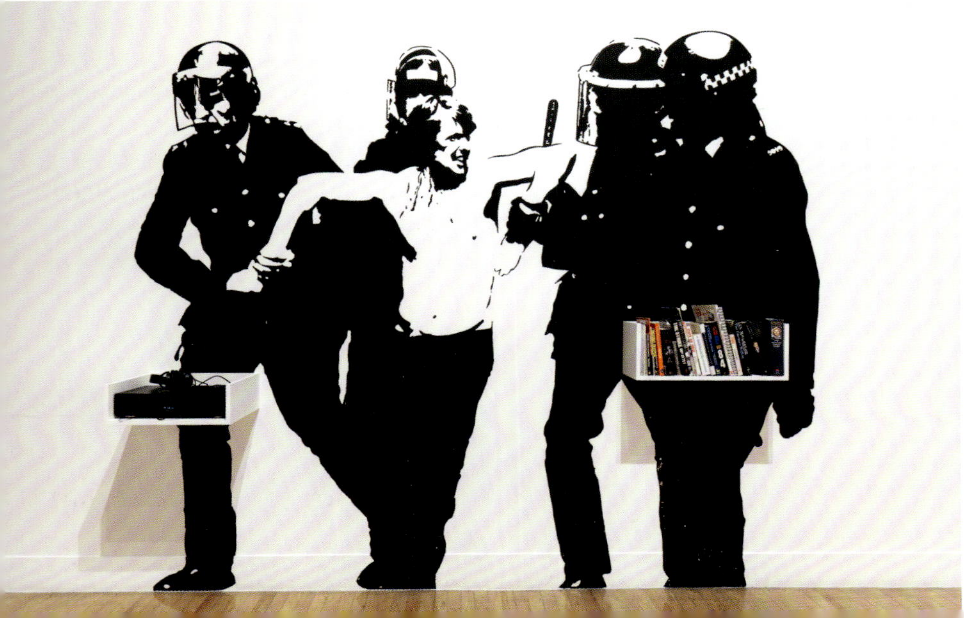

The Battle of Orgreave Archive (An Injury to One is an Injury to All) 2001, Wall painting, paint on fibreboard, vinyl text, map, books, jacket, shield, printed papers; two videos; video, projection, colour and sound,62 min Dimensions variable

Why would you restage a battle? The concept of re-enactments usually conjures up images of actors who are not necessarily history enthusiasts, but more interested in dressing up and hitting each other with sticks. Deller, ever the politico, took the fresh and painful memory of the Battle of Orgreave and thrust it into contemporary memory. The violent confrontation that took place in 1984 between police and miners outside a coking plant (where coal is purified) at Orgreave in South Yorkshire was one of the tipping points during the Miners' Strike of 1984–5. Deller's recreation, an event staged and filmed in the very same village just seventeen years later, saw many relatives of former miners as well as re-enactment specialists revisit the riotous affair. The film, along with a rich archive of accompanying research materials, forms a compelling, nuanced installation that insists on the remembrance of this pivotal event, explores this moment of revolt and demands better for the future. The work's subtitle underpins the message, 'an injury to one is an injury to all', a slogan popularised by the Industrial Workers of the World (IWW), or Wobblies, and adopted by many other unions since. In his restaging in a fashion usually reserved for medieval battles and war recreations, Deller shines light on the resemblance between this moment and civil war. Deller's *The Battle of Orgreave Archive* becomes more than just a recreation of an event; it represents the destruction of mining communities, as well as the wider social fabric of the working classes, under Margaret Thatcher's government.

Jeremy Deller
b.1966

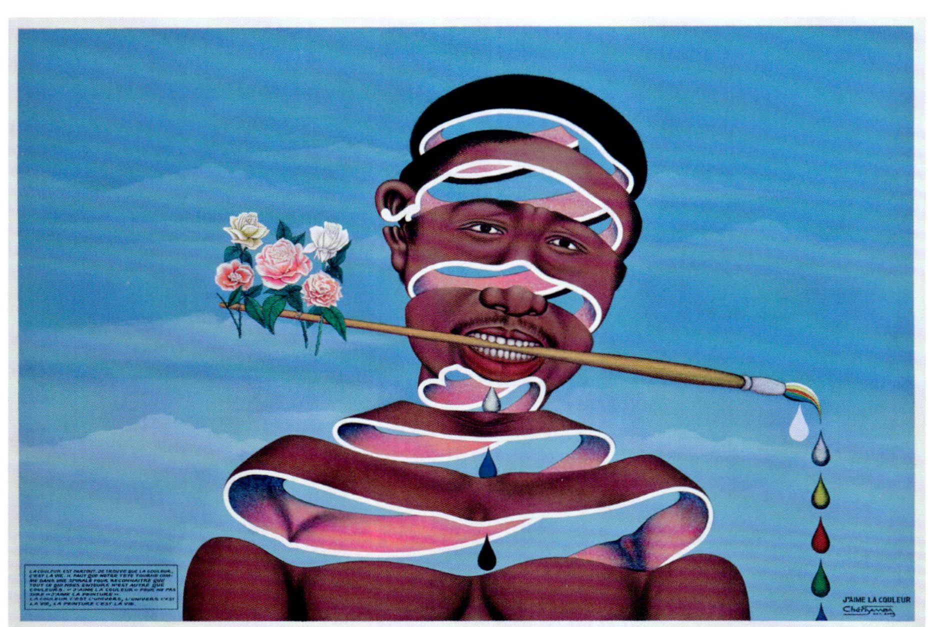

LA COULEUR EST PARTOUT. JE TROUVE QUE LA COULEUR, C'EST LA VIE. IL FAUT QUE NOTRE TÊTE TOURNE COMME DANS UNE SPIRALE POUR RECONNAÎTRE QUE TOUT CE QUI NOUS ENTOURE N'EST AUTRE QUE COULEURS. « J'AIME LA COULEUR » POUR NE PAS DIRE « J'AIME LA PEINTURE ». LA COULEUR C'EST L'UNIVERS, L'UNIVERS C'EST LA VIE, LA PEINTURE C'EST LA VIE.
J'AIME LA COULEUR
Chéri Samba

In the latter half of the 1950s, a wave of independence swept throughout Africa. The continent, previously divided up and exploited by Imperialism, was fighting to regain its identity. This required courageous political leaders and, in the tumultuous process, the need to exorcise the pain, strength and hope of the ever-changing times found itself in the capable hands of the newly emerging Zaire Popular School of Painting, founded by Chéri Samba in the 1970s. One of Africa's best-known artists, Samba mixes humour with truth to advocate for change. His work unveils the political, cultural and economic realities of living in Zaire (now the Democratic Republic of Congo) and life in Kinshasa, commenting on social inequalities and corruption, as well as sexuality and popular culture. He searches for shock, and hands it to you in the unassuming visual language of billboards and murals. His work is a pictorial embodiment of the socio-political reality of his lived experience. At the age of sixteen, he left his father, a blacksmith, and mother, a farmer, and nine siblings to work in Kinshasa and to prove that paintings can open eyes and send powerful messages to the world. Originally working on sackcloth, instead of the more costly canvas, he borrowed elements from his work as a comic-strip artist, such as speech bubbles, to emphasise his narrative intentions and introduce his socio-political commentary to the compositions. Text features heavily in his paintings; it demands time and reflection, rather than a casual glance. Samba's *J'aime la couleur* series – undoubtedly his most well-known body of work – is an unabashed celebration of colour that depicts Samba himself as an unravelling spiral – a self-portrait as a lifeline of humanity and a dissection of what it means to be human.

Chéri Samba
b.1956

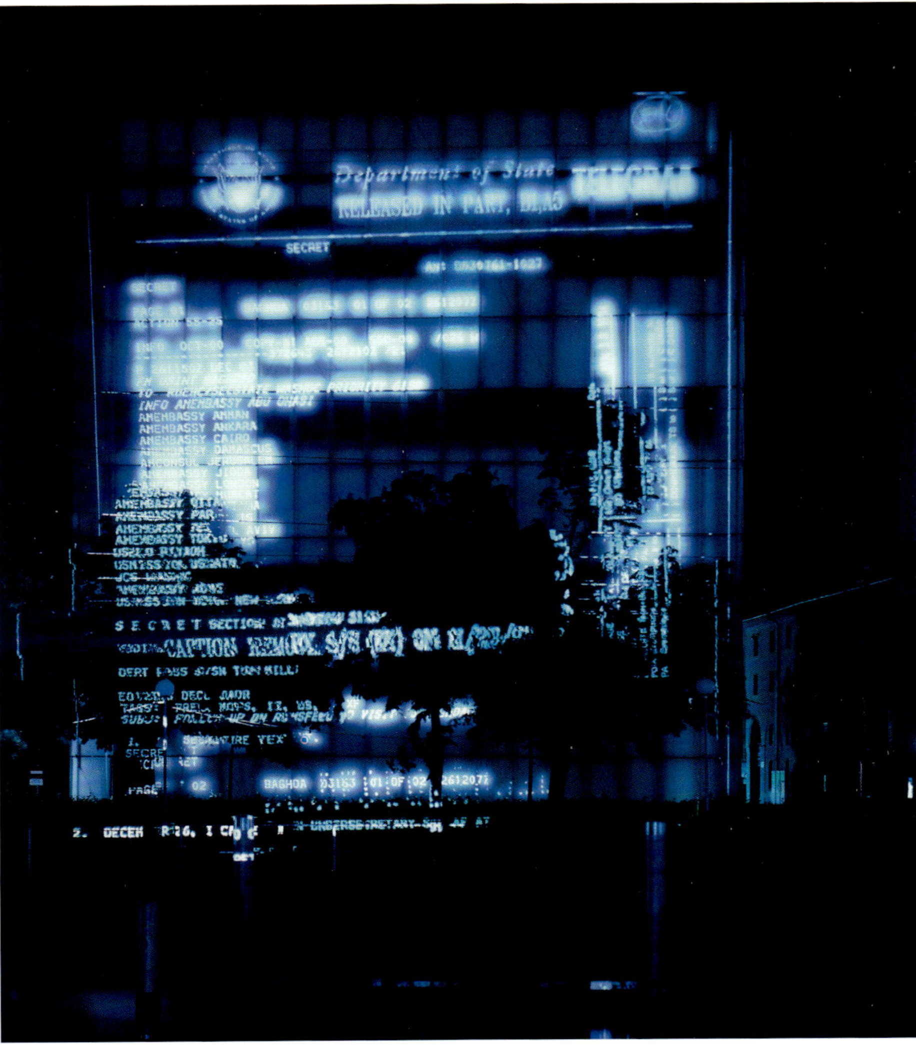
Department of State
RELEASED IN PART, B1,A5
SECRET
SECRET SECTION
CAPTION REMOVED S/S (EO) ON
DEPT PASS S/SN TOM KELLY
E.O. DECL OADR
SUBJ: FOLLOW UP ON RUMSFELD TO VISIT
BAGHDAD 03163 01 OF 02 2612077
2. DECEM R 16, I CAL E N UNDERSECRETARY S I AF AT

Jenny Holzer has been illuminating the night with her poetic text projections since 1991. Indeed, the artist does with her art what the broadsheets and other media no longer seem capable of: when her light meets a surface it seeks to recover the truth. Whether questioning humanity's consumerist impulses, describing torture or lamenting the tragedy of death, Holzer's use of language and familiar digital aesthetics forces contemplation. At its most subversive, it blends in among the noise of advertisements and violates our expectations. Firmly rooted in the digital age, her canvases take the form of all manner of surfaces, which she then illuminates with her powerful decrees.

In 2004, Holzer utilised her signature 'Xenon' film projectors – which she has been using since 1966 to cast monumental images and text, including her *Truisms* (a series of insightful and zesty one-liners; 1977–), in light on the sides of buildings and landscapes around the world, for a new purpose. From 10pm to 1am every night between 11 and 18 June, Holzer projected a series of extracts from the National Security Archive's declassified documents in various locations in Austria, including the façade of the Kunsthaus Bregenz, the Rhomberg rock quarry, the Vermunt reservoir dam and the *West Side Story* floating stage on Lake Constance. The extracts, which included more than thirty former national secrets primarily relating to US foreign policy in the Middle East, were obtained from the National Security Archive by the Freedom of Information Act. Once classified, now public record but heavily redacted, they detail the political debates unfolding during the presidencies of Ronald Reagan, George H.W. Bush, Bill Clinton and George W. Bush concerning international trade in arms and oil, the war on terrorism, 9/11, the FBI and CIA and Congress's oversight of the intelligence community. *Xenon* is a razor-sharp enlightenment that is both a critique of our time and poetic musing on humanity.

Jenny Holzer
b.1950

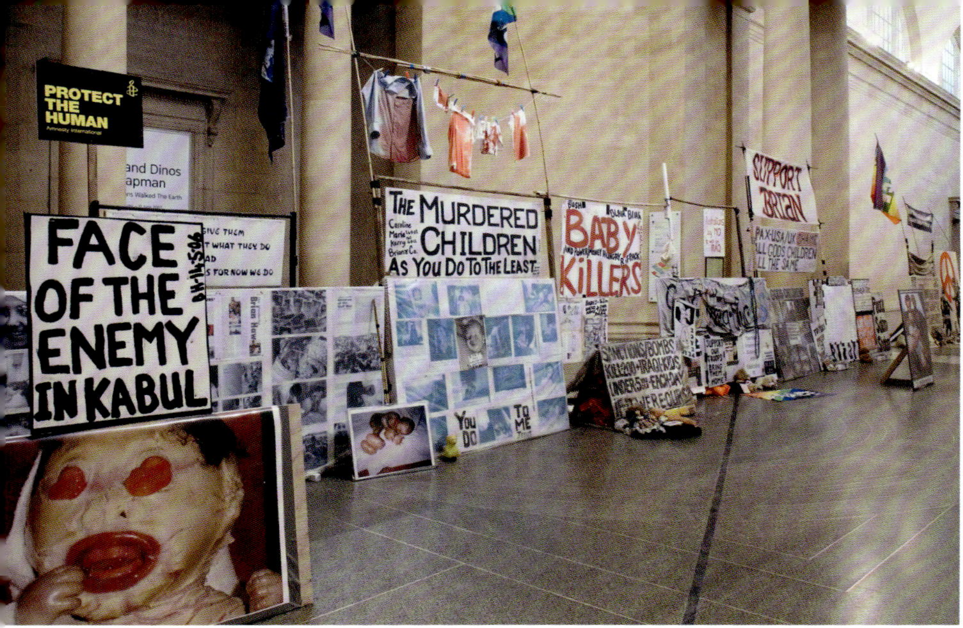

PROTECT THE HUMAN
Amnesty International

and Dinos
...apman
...ns Walked The Earth

FACE OF THE ENEMY IN KABUL

The MURDERED CHILDREN
Caroline
Marie and
Kerry and
Brian & Co.
As You Do To The Least...

BABY KILLERS

SUPPORT BRIAN
PAX USA/UK
ALL GODS CHILDREN
ALL THE SAME

You DO TO ME

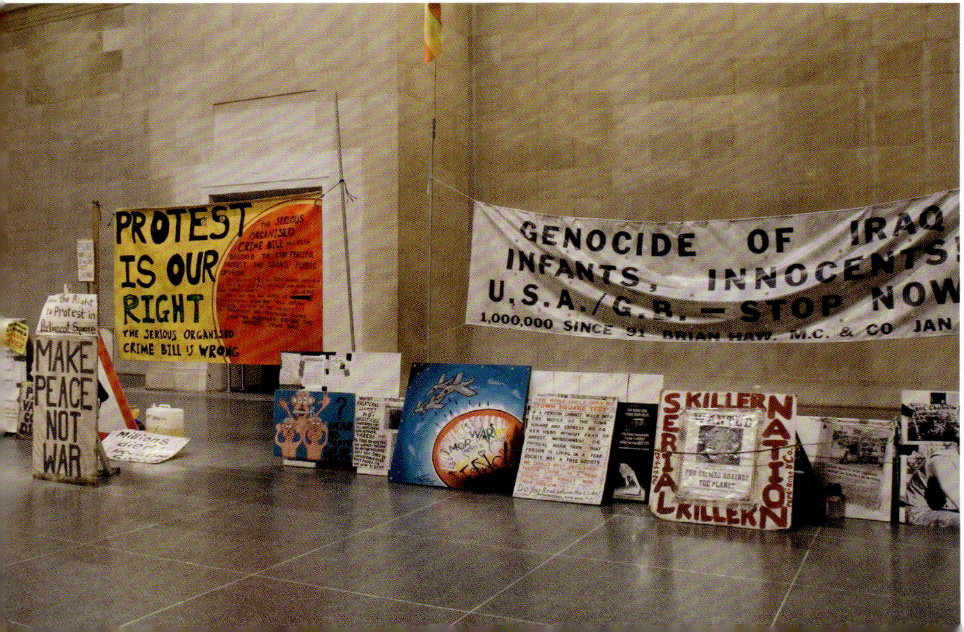

PROTEST IS OUR RIGHT
THE SERIOUS ORGANISED
CRIME BILL IS WRONG

MAKE PEACE NOT WAR

Millions

GENOCIDE OF IRAQ
INFANTS, INNOCENTS
U.S.A./G.B. – STOP NOW
1,000,000 SINCE 91 BRIAN HAW M.C. & CO JAN

SERIAL KILLER NATION

State Britain
2007, Wood,
hardboard,
cardboard,
fabric, paint,
printed paper,
photographs and
other materials
Dimensions
variable

Walking into the Duveen Galleries of Tate Britain in spring 2007, you'd have been forgiven for being taken aback. *State Britain* saw artist Mark Wallinger recreate the protest camp set up by peace campaigner Brian Haw in Parliament Square, London, in 2001. Wallinger spared no detail, and he meticulously reconstructed more than 600 weather-beaten banners, peace flags and messages of encouragement, mapping the five years that Haw dedicated to the cause. In Wallinger's restaging, Haw's protest becomes art with a capital A, but it was art in its inception. It speaks the same language as all good art – it advocates for change. In addition to the hand-painted placards and teddy bears wearing T-shirts emblazoned with peace slogans, Wallinger even went so far as remaking with complete attention to detail Haw's makeshift tarpaulin shelter and tea-making area. Staged as one long line, 43 metres in length, it perfectly mirrors the site opposite the Houses of Parliament where Haw's protest camp held ground. Haw created the art, Wallinger made us realise it was art. Protest is like a readymade; it deserves contemplation.

Mark Wallinger
b.1959

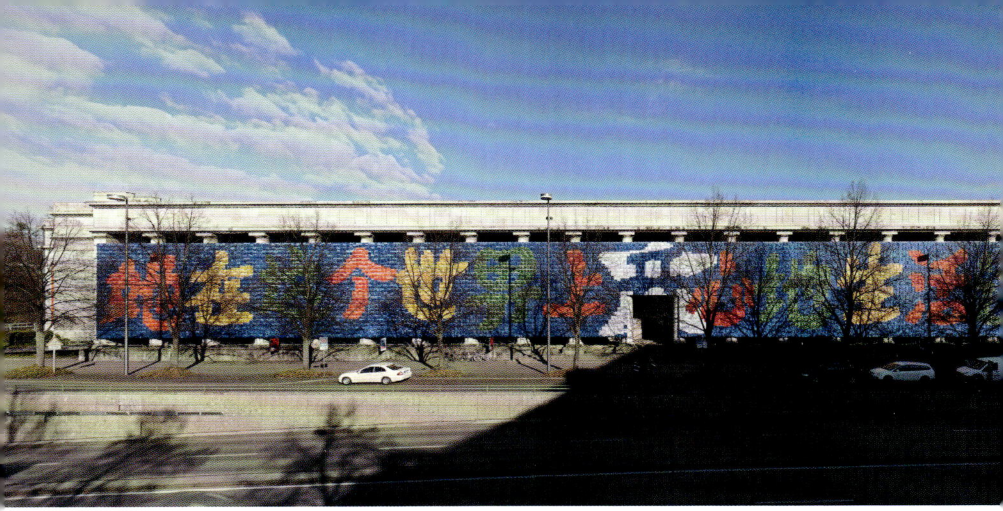

Remembering 2009
Installation
view at the
Haus der Kunst,
Munich

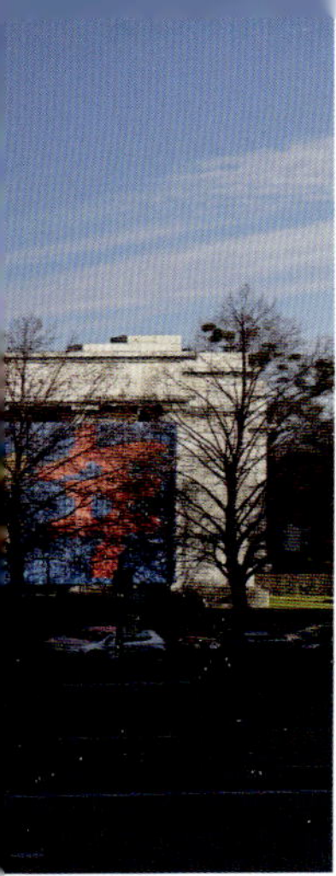

There are times when political art can be dangerous for its maker. In 2009, Ai Weiwei created a work to honour the thousands of children who had died in an earthquake in the central region of Sichuan, China. The 2008 earthquake killed almost 70,000 citizens, including many schoolchildren.

The Chinese government censored information about the event, so the details of what really happened are unclear. Ai Weiwei took the investigation into his own hands, contacting educational, police and civil departments to ensure that neither the children nor the devastation would be forgotten. His Citizens' Investigation was comprised of volunteers whose purpose was to account for the total number of casualties and to seek an explanation for this destruction and the loss of so many young lives. To articulate his discoveries, he listed all the victims on his blog. The blog was eventually shut down, but the never-relenting artist did not back down. In a dramatic political act for his forthcoming show in Haus der Kunst, Munich, he covered the façade of the museum in 9,000 bright primary-coloured backpacks, arranged to read as a quote from one of the victim's mothers. She had said to the artist: 'All I want is to let the world remember she had been living happily for seven years.' *Remembering*, bold and unmissable above the entrance of the building, became a symbol of a protest against censorship and a beacon of hope for those families whose children had been lost.

In 2011, Ai Weiwei was arrested in China, following a crackdown by the government on 'political dissidents' (a term used to classify those who seek to subvert state power). His criticisms of the Chinese government's corruption, neglect for human rights and lack of freedom of speech and thought put the artist in grave danger.

Ai Weiwei
b.1957

What do fire hoses, the material used to create this piece, have to do with protest? The title, *Civil Tapestry 4*, points directly to the work's political content.

In May 1963, a group of Black children and students marched in Birmingham, Alabama, for equal rights for Black people in America. Their rally, known as the Children's Crusade, was met with violence, as the Birmingham Commissioner of Public Safety ordered the police to spray the crowd with water from fire hoses to break up the march. The blasts hit the children with such brutal force that many were injured. The subsequent public condemnation of this outrageous event was a turning point in the civil rights movement.

Fire hoses, as Gates presents them, are therefore politically charged; they represent the violence used to intimidate those who speak out. They also suggest other terrible moments, such as the destruction of Black churches by fire, and specifically the bombing of the Sixteenth Street Baptist Church in Birmingham in September 1963. Gates stitches together the hoses to create a homage to the material that, at the hands of police, sought to end civil unrest, but which instead actioned what the protests were demanding: equal rights. In one fell swoop, that which sought to silence with violence gave voice to the unheard.

Gates also questions the symbolic history of these water carriers in his earlier probing and moving work, *Minority Majority* 2002. Using hoses as his medium to reference police violence against peaceful protestors throughout history, Gates also explores how raw materials can hold and embody history, even when abstracted or transformed: in the case of *Minority Majority*, into a pseudo-American flag. The title of the piece reflects the changes that were happening culturally during its conception, and how the minority/majority status was shifting. It acknowledges this by bringing to light other corners of the past and specifically

Next page:
Civil Tapestry 4
2011, Fire hoses,
vinyl and wood
182.9 × 487.7

America's history, and using the iconic symbol of Americanness to do so. It is a reminder that the land of the free and home of the brave refers to only one part of American citizenry; the rest have long since been rallying for freedom and have been brave in the face of injustice. Gates, using the physical material and relics of protest, questions how we view things and how we hold subjective history close to our chest while encouraging us to look and think a little longer.

Both *Minority Majority* and *Civil Tapestry 4* are at once moving tributes, a reminder of the personal and physical risk of protest, and testament to its lasting power to move people and evoke change. This woven wake-up call reminds us of how far we have come – though we still have a way to go – and how the most unassuming of objects can have extreme political portent.

Theaster Gates
b.1973

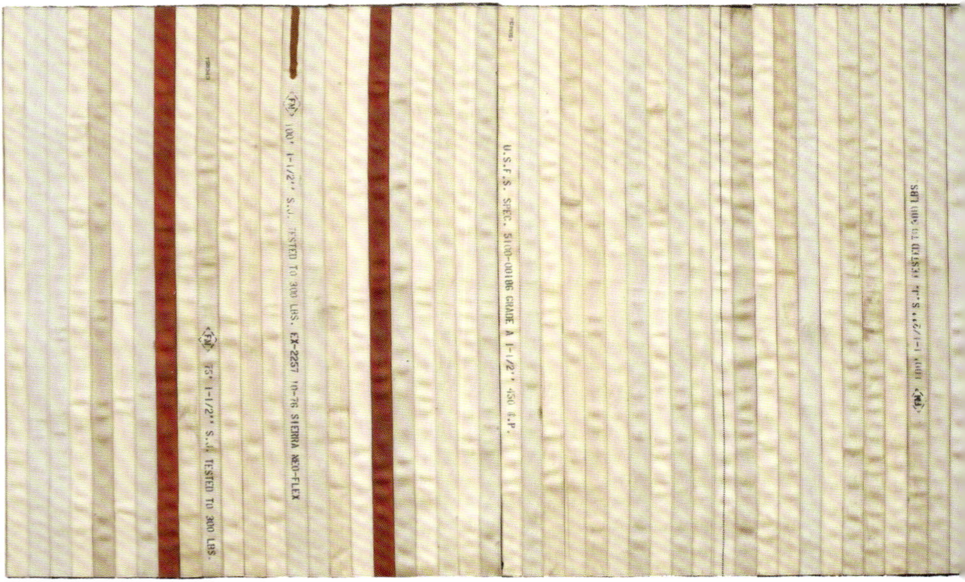

(FM) 100' 1-1/2'' S.J. TESTED TO 300 LBS.
U.S.F.S. SPEC. 5100-00186 GRADE A 1-1/2'' 450 G.P.
(FM) 100' 1-1/2'' S.J. TESTED TO 300 LBS. EX-2257 10-76 SIERRA NEO-FLEX
(FM) 75' 1-1/2'' S.J. TESTED TO 300 LBS.

75' 1-1/2'' S.J. TESTED TO 300 LBS.
50' 1-1/2'' S.J. TESTED TO 500 LBS.
75' 1-1/2'' S.J. TESTED TO 300 LBS., EX-2257 9-74
50' 1-1/2'' S.J. TESTED TO 300 LBS., 6-75
(FM) 75' 1-1/2'' S.J. TESTED TO 300 LBS.
U.S.F.S. SPEC. 5100-00186 GRADE A 1-1/2'' 450 W.P. N.F.H. 6-76
75' 1-1/2'' S.J. TESTED TO 300 LBS.
EX-2257 9-75

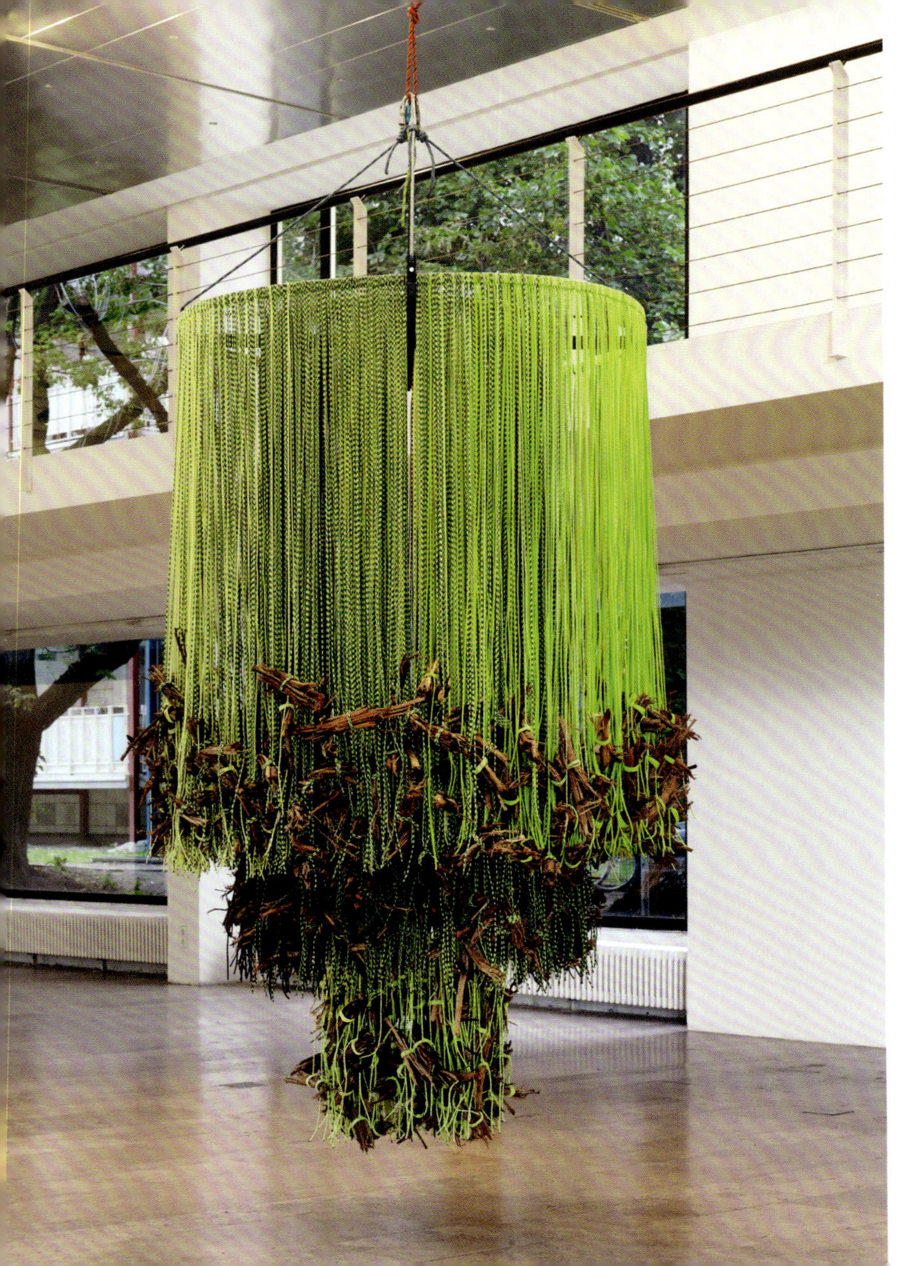

Andrea Bowers makes art that campaigns for gender equality and environmentalism. *Memorial to Arcadia Woodlands Clear-Cut (Green, Violet and Brown)* is a hanging sculpture of cords and wood. The artwork began in 2011 when Bowers, along with three other activists, was arrested for her attempt to save a forest of trees in Arcadia, California. After her release, Bowers returned to the site of the clear-cut and found huge piles of chipped wood – all the oaks and sycamores had met a tree-chipper fate – and a landscape that was nothing more than a barren dirt patch. The trees had been ripped out of the woodlands so that the area could be turned into a dumping ground for dirt and debris scraped from the bottom of the concrete LA river network. This work, full of pathos, is a protest to protect our last areas of urban wilderness. Bowers filled her truck with wood chips and was compelled to use them to memorialise and monumentalise the trees in her sculpture. Woven from the stumps and logs, it evolved into a huge, hanging chandelier composed from the detritus of an event protestors sought to prevent. Bower turns protest on its head by making the materials of the event have living value as an ongoing protest to inspire future action. It is ethereal, and transcendental; it inspires awe as much as it provokes. Memorials serve many purposes; remembrance of a moment but, pushing that idea further, ensuring that tragic events are not forgotten and so not repeated. That which is remembered is seen by the public as important. If we memorialise nature, does that help us to understand why we need to protect it? This is protest without picket signs.

Andrea Bowers
b.1965

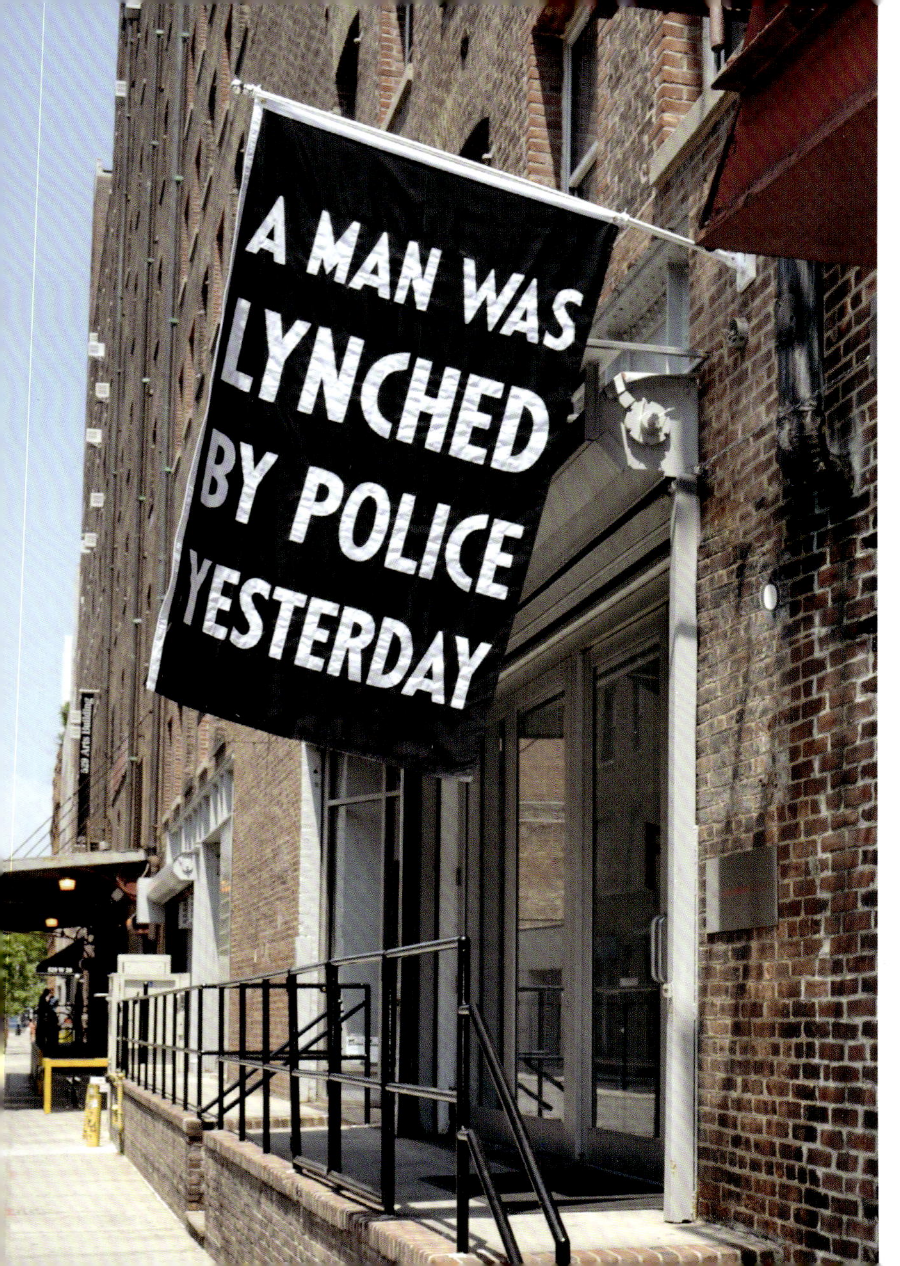

A MAN WAS LYNCHED BY POLICE YESTERDAY

Simplicity can hit you hard. The stark, white text on a black banner, printed with the words 'a man was lynched by police yesterday', is a refashioning by the artist Dread Scott of the iconic flag that, in the 1920s and 1930s, the NAACP (The National Association for the Advancement of Colored People) flew from the window in its New York headquarters the day after someone was lynched, as part of its anti-lynching campaign. Lynching, recurrent in the Jim Crow era – Jim Crow was a character popularised by Thomas Dartmouth White in his act 'Jump, Jim Crow', a moniker that later became synonmyous with Black people, and which was adopted in the language of racist legislation – was the public, and also publicised, legal torture and murder of Black people. It was a very real threat that loomed over the everyday lives of Black people, as it was a fate that could be catalysed by any or, indeed, no reason, at any time. Sound familiar? After the murder of George Floyd in 2020, the world woke up to the plight of police brutality, as the circulation of video footage made wilful ignorance implausible. This artwork presents a poignant *déjà vu* and was created in response to events in 2015, when fork-lift operator Walter Scott died after being shot in the back by a police officer. The phrase has been repeated on placards of those protesting police brutality, particularly at the protests following the murder of George Floyd. Scott has cast the police force as twentieth-century lynchers of victims once hung, now shot – the methods change but the senseless reasoning of prejudice runs throughout. Scott's work looks at how the past sets the stage for the present, but also calls for change in the future. Representing a past that still haunts the present, the artwork has come to represent police brutality and the racially motivated deaths of Black people. It harnesses the visual language of protest and puts reality in very plain terms that we cannot ignore. Its call for the end of terror is direct and potent.

Dread Scott
b.1965

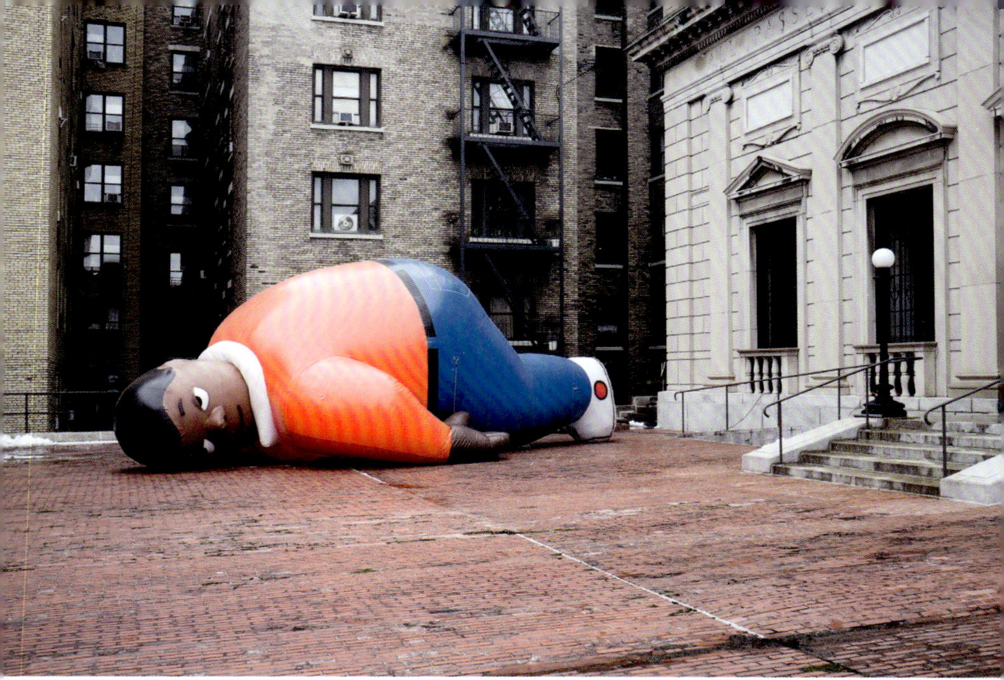

Sanford Biggers's *Laocoön* is an enormous inflatable figure of Bill Cosby's animated schoolyard hero, Fat Albert. Though humorously large, it holds a dark, deflated message, as the figure lies down with his eyeballs rolled to the back of his head. Adding further potency, air is gently pumped into the body – as it expands and contracts, it simulates breathing; or, rather, a shallow, laboured, exasperated struggle for air. The title of the work references the figure of Laocoön from Virgil's *Aeneid*, who is killed after an attempt to spear the Trojan Horse, as well as the famed ancient sculpture *Laocoön and His Sons*, the subjects of which are shown writhing away from attacking serpents. The expressive and tragic possibilities of the ancient work of art are mirrored by the contemporary politics framing *Laocoön*.

The work was unveiled during Art Basel Miami in 2015, a powerful and shocking display for the blue-chip bourgeoisie. Reports of police brutality had become so commonplace by that time that they were woven into the fabric of daily life; Biggers makes this fact big, bold and impossible to miss, and all the more harrowing in light of the deaths of Michael Brown and Eric Garner at the hands of the police in 2014, as well as countless other Black men – 1,134 in 2015, five times higher than the number of their white counterparts – who were killed by police officers in the year of the work's conception. It is a brave protest that resonates now as it did then. It is a protest not against a single tragedy, but to an undulating, unrelenting injustice we still seek to overcome.

Sanford Biggers
b.1970

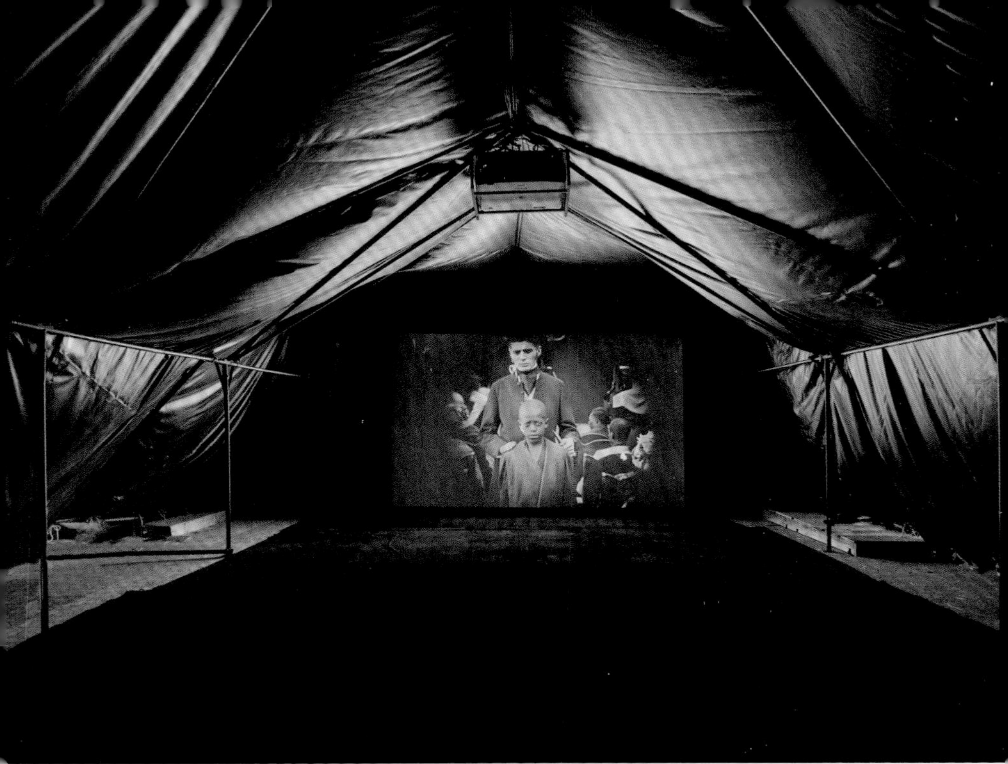

Love is
the Message,
The Message
is Death
2016, Video,
projection,
colour and
sound (stereo)
7 min 33 sec

Arthur Jafa's *Love is the Message, The Message is Death* is a battle cry in moving image. It hits you in the gut. The piercing highs and lows of Kanye West's gospel-meets-hip-hop track 'Ultralight Beam' become a moving musical background to Jafa's masterful collage of found footage mined from the archives. Watermarked photographs of civil rights leaders and grainy YouTube videos of sweaty bodies bumping and grinding, are intricately woven in this seven-minute video with reflections on historic events, and the personal experiences of everyday African Americans, whose anonymous bodies are shown both desecrated and delighted. In its densely compacted nature, *Love is the Message* shakes you out of complacency; it calls for you to rub your eyes and really look at the world in which we live. In reclaiming modes of communication – press footage, news reportage, community video (a prolific movement in the 1970s and 1980s), music videos – Jafa proclaims that if it is the media that damns us, then let media be our redemption. Seeing the LA riots from a helicopter vantage point, a scene quickly interspliced with well-known Black icons, the viewer keeps their breath baited, and watery eyes on the brink. It is a challenge to watch this film and not be moved.

Arthur Jafa
b.1960

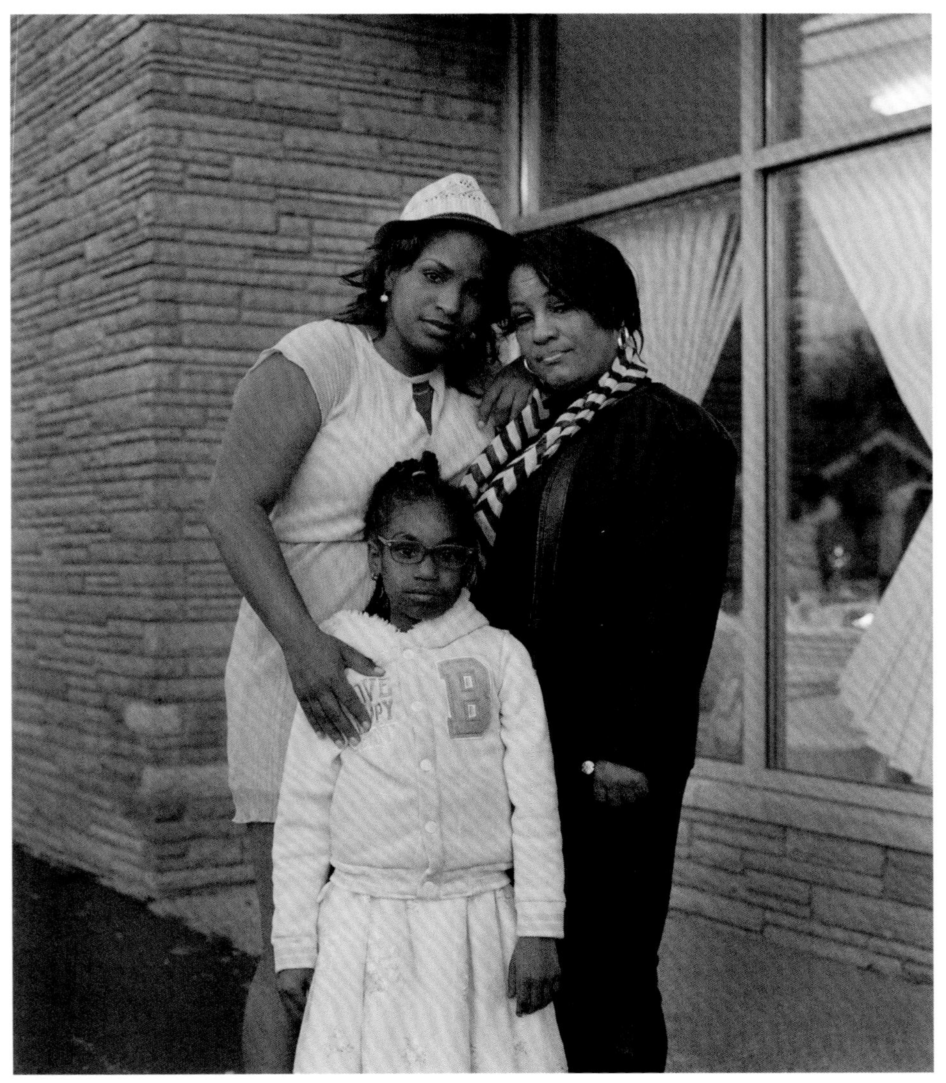

This moving photographic series uses the power of documentary to inform and protest the water crisis in Flint, Michigan. The residents of Flint are mostly poor, with forty per cent coming from impoverished communities. In 2013, the Flint City Council voted to leave the expensive Detroit water system and its contract with the Karegnondi Water Authority (KWA), a water-distribution corporation. As an interim water source, and to save money, Flint started to draw water from the 126-km Flint River, which flows from Lapeer County into Saginaw Bay. Soon after, complaints came in, noting the water's rancid taste and smell, and the residents' resulting severe skin conditions, and hair – including eyelashes – falling out.

The Flint River had been shrouded in rumour for decades, with many suspecting that it was a dumping site for toxic waste and chemicals. In the 1930s, when thousands of fish died at once, a lab determined that pollution had so deoxygenated the water that the fish had suffocated to death. Four months after officials opened the city's taps to Flint River water, tests detected traces of E. coli.

The series *Flint is Family* saw the artist spend five months in Flint living with three generations of women – the poet Shea Cobb, her mother Renée, and her daughter Zion – observing their day-to-day lives as they endured one of the most devastating ecological disasters in US history. It is a powerful social documentary, and became a platform to advocate for others; the oppressed, the disenfranchised. Frazier's valiant documentation and humanising of the Flint population drew attention to the issue and made the afflictions of many personal, and so harder to ignore. By portraying the daily struggles of the Cobb family, Frazier created a powerful story about the impact of a systemic problem disproportionately affecting marginalised communities. The crisis ended in 2019, but not before up to 12,000 children were exposed to lead, and a public state of emergency was declared. And the effects linger on.

LaToya Ruby Frazier
b.1982

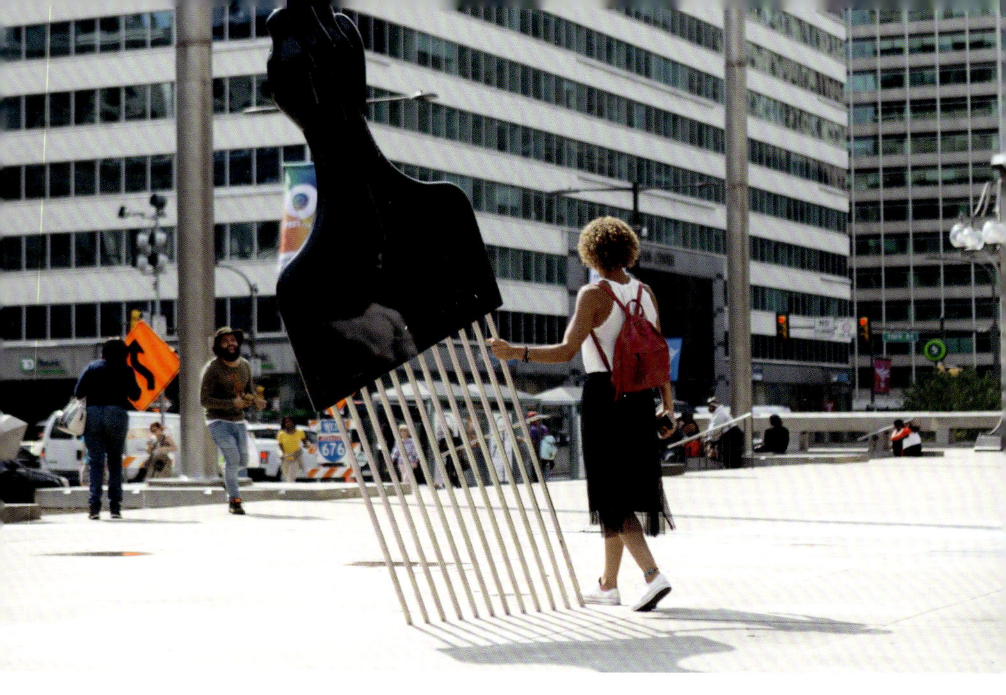

All Power to All People 2017
Aluminium and stainless steel
Installed as part of *Monument Lab*, Mural Arts Philadelphia, Thomas Paine Plaza, Philadelphia, PA, 19 September 2017

In 2017 American artist Hank Willis Thomas erected a giant Afro hair pick in Thomas Paine Plaza, right across from Philadelphia City Hall. Standing at 2.4 m tall, the hair pick was a powerful public intervention – a political symbol emblematic of a community and collective identity lacking representation throughout America, at a grand scale. The work echoes the monumentalising of everyday objects by pop artist Claes Oldenburg (b.1929), but triumphs in the fusing of the Black Power salute, and what it signifies, into a hair pick. The Afro has always been political; synonymous with the Black Panther movement, it also represents a celebration of diversity that white supremacy sought to quell. At the hands of Hank Willis Thomas, it becomes a symbol of resistance to oppression, and a call to place new ideas, relating to community, strength and diversity in our public spaces. Why are there more statues that memorialise figures who perpetuated violence and inequality than those that commemorate community, comradeship, perseverance and togetherness?

Artists effect social change. Another version of this sculpture has toured around the United States since 2018, and undoubtedly played a role in maintaining the momentum of the ongoing protests for racial equity throughout 2020, while offering a platform for civic leaders and activists to be heard. Art like this riles us up and makes us ask questions about the world in which we live. Who would have thought a giant comb could do so much?

Hank Willis Thomas
b.1976

What can we do to enrich our community? Art as a mechanism to reshape social structure made its first strong appearance in the 1970s with German conceptual artist Joseph Beuys (1921–86), who coined the phrase 'social sculpture'. Beuys's theory was that everything in the social realm is art, and so every corner of our lives can be approached in a creative way. His investigations into social sculpture and the role that communities can play in their own development had marginalised communities – their regeneration and socio-political engagement – as its main concern.

Houston's Third Ward is home to arguably one of the most impressive and visionary social sculptures in America. *Project Row Houses* (PRH) was founded in 1993 and is headed by Rick Lowe and a group of African American artists (James Bettison, Bert Long Jr., Jesse Lott, Floyd Newsum, Bert Samples and George Smit) who foster and encourage creativity, as well as providing a platform for change and visual protest. The culture and history of the Third Ward in Houston, Texas reflects the strong African American presence at its core, which can be tracked to the early nineteenth century. Initially, there was a fairly even split between white and African American populations, until the 1930s, when middle-class African American communities were predominant until the 1980s, after which the community began to decline, catalysed by disinvestment as the cocaine epidemic hit. In 1993, seven African American artists and neighbours saw twenty-two shotgun-style row houses and in that, saw an opportunity. The shotgun house is an import from West Africa, via the slave trade; working-class African Americans swiftly adopted this model and built these houses in the Third Ward. They are small houses with a floorplan that offers an unobstructed view from the front door through to the back door. The artists rescued the houses from demolition with the idea to use them to promote social transformation. The work is undoubtedly inspired by the work of John Biggers, an African-American muralist who came to prominence after the Second World War, and who portrayed the shotgun row house as a community asset, but also Beuys's thinking around social sculpture. The houses become exhibition sites, too. During the twice-yearly 'Rounds', local and international artists respond to themes at the heart of the neighbourhood, such as gentrification, Black motherhood, and perseverance. The exteriors of the houses are also emblazoned, in colourful revolt, with bold phrases such as 'WHAT WASHINGTON NEEDS IS ADULT SUPERVISION'. Important reminders about the ethos of the project can be found in other phrases that appear, such as 'WE ARE THE PEOPLE' or 'YOU GOTTA LOVE US OR LEAVE US ALONE'. The project expanded to a non-profit organisation with a mission to preserve the history, culture, and traditional buildings of the northern Third Ward through art and affordable rental housing. *Project Row Houses* encourages us to look beyond beautifying spaces and gentrification, and rather, using the resources at hand, respond, with the poetry of the materials of the place, and use this as protest and political commentary. It is a leading example of what art can do: it can delve into the fields of community development and historical and cultural preservation, empowering people to see themselves in a different way. The three pillars of PRH, and of social sculpture, are art, community and neighbourhood. This social sculpture tracks, memorialises, archives and reflects the ever-changing socio-politics of the community, while providing a site of grief, solace and hope. Art can be a protest for a better tomorrow, but it can also bring people together; this is a great example of that.

Rick Lowe
b.1961

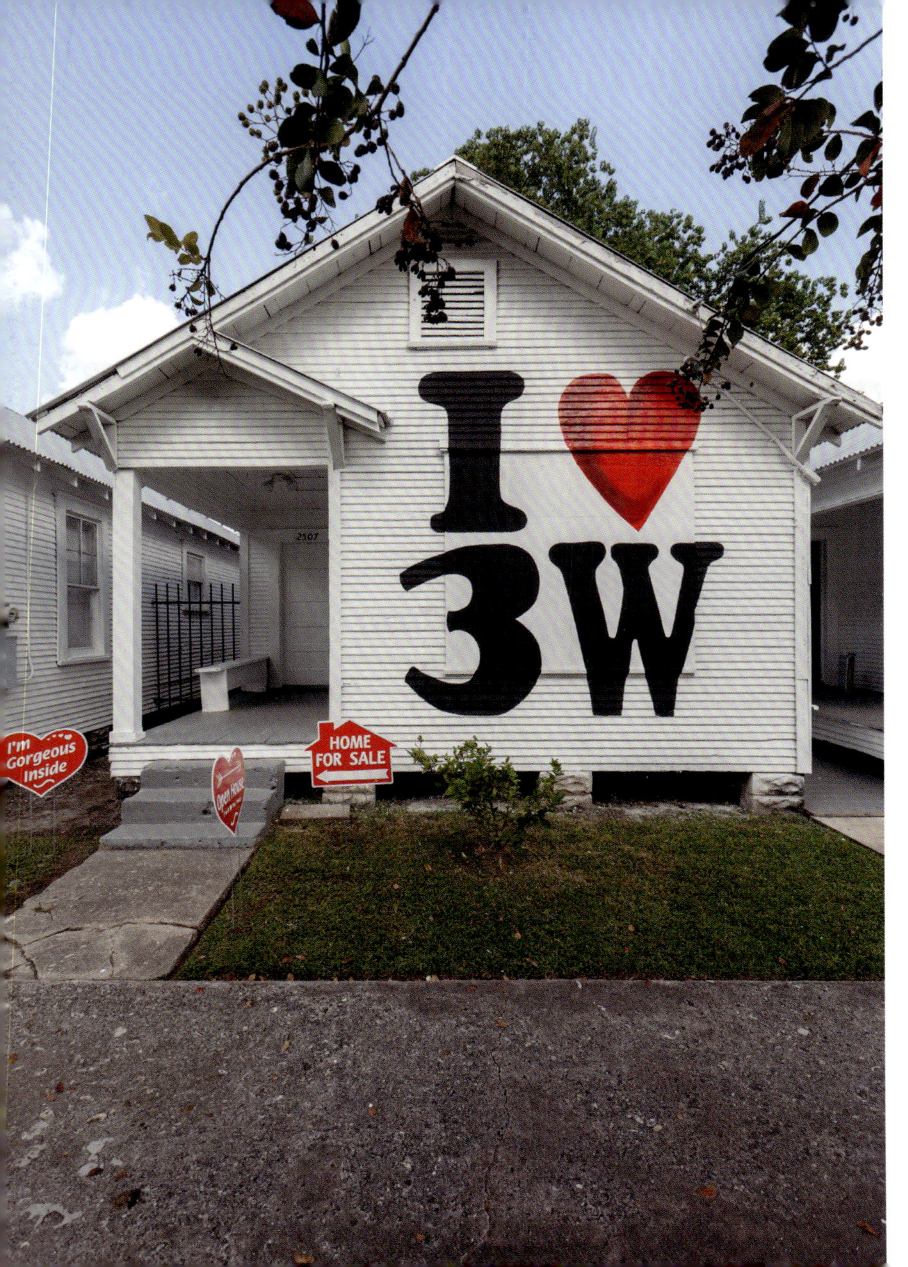

I ♥ 3W
I'm Gorgeous Inside
Open House
HOME FOR SALE

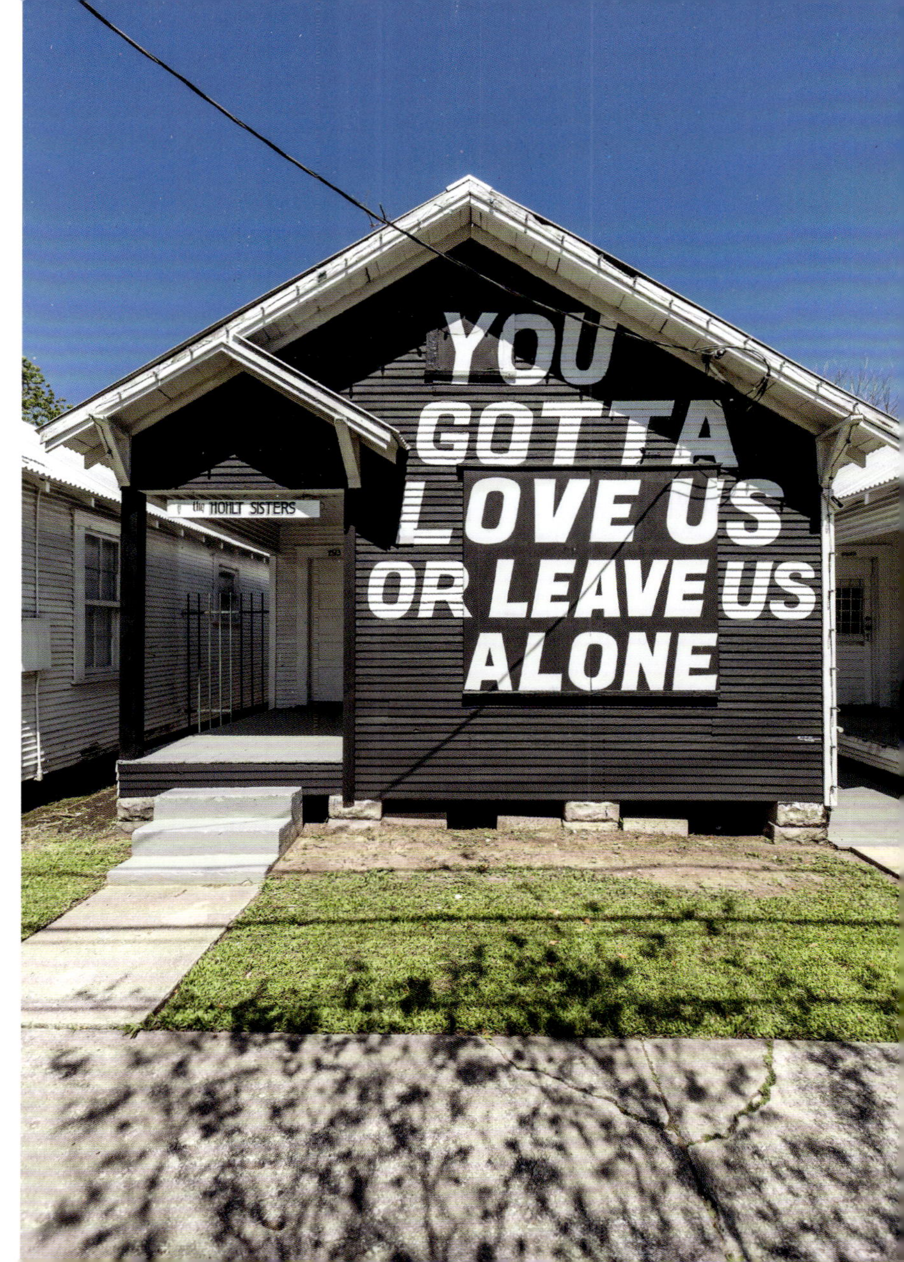
the MOILT SISTERS
YOU
GOTTA
LOVE US
OR LEAVE US
ALONE

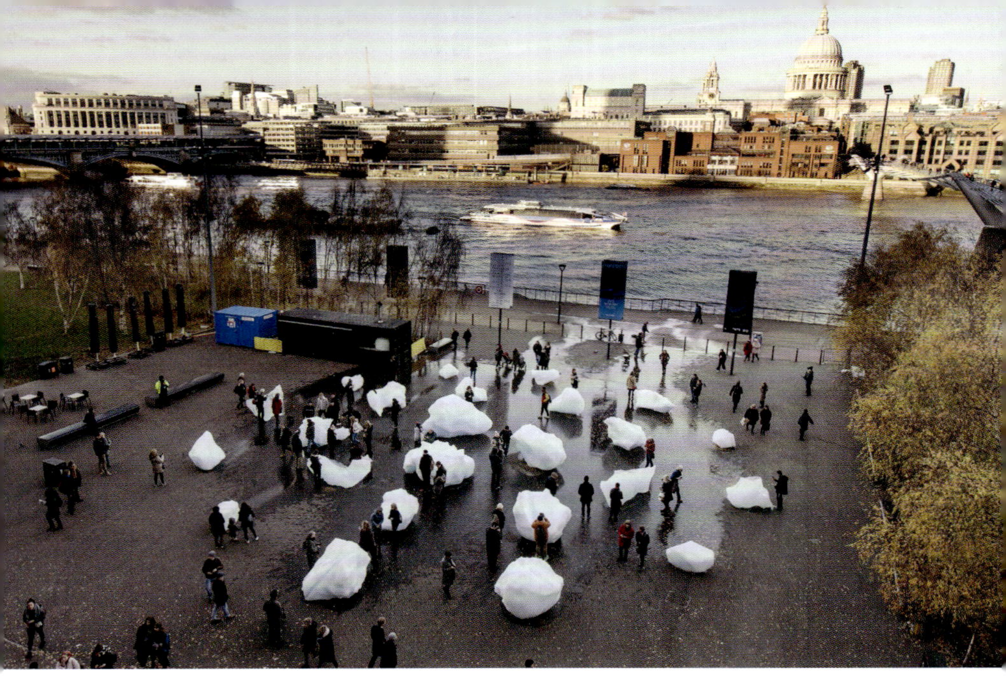

Ice Watch 2018
Supported
by Bloomberg
Installation
outside Tate
Modern, London

Does public art have the power to inspire action against climate change? Or is it a waste of energy? If you had been walking along the South Bank or preparing to visit Tate Modern in December 2018, you may well have been advised to look out for ice. Not that it was hard to miss. *Ice Watch* was an installation by the artist Olafur Eliasson, which comprised twenty-four glacial ice blocks, each weighing between 1.5 and 5 tonnes, arranged in a circle in front of the gallery. Jagged white hunks of ice and translucent slices and shards also appeared in front of the Bloomberg offices in London's Square Mile. This wasn't the first time such a quantity of ice found itself in the most unusual of locations: it was the third instalment of Eliasson's *Ice Watch* series, previously iterated in Copenhagen in 2014 and Paris in 2015. Together with geologist Minik Rosing, Eliasson fished the ice blocks from the Nuup Kangerlua fjord in Greenland as they started to melt into the sea and shipped them to London in freezers usually reserved for frozen prawns. In *Ice Watch* Eliasson draws attention to the global climate crisis; something that he does with exceptional timing – like the earlier works, this 2018 installation in London coincided with a global environment event, namely the meeting of world leaders at the COP24 Climate Change Conference in Katowice, Poland. As the ice melted away, minute by minute, over the duration of the installation, the urgency of the climate crisis was laid bare. Reading about glaciers melting is quite different to seeing them disappearing in front of our very eyes, on the streets we walk every day. *Ice Watch* is a powerful fusing of public art and political action; a staunch reminder of the effects of environmental crises that will remain in the minds of many well after the ice finally melted and evaporated away.

Olafur Eliasson & Minik Rosing
b.1967 & 1957

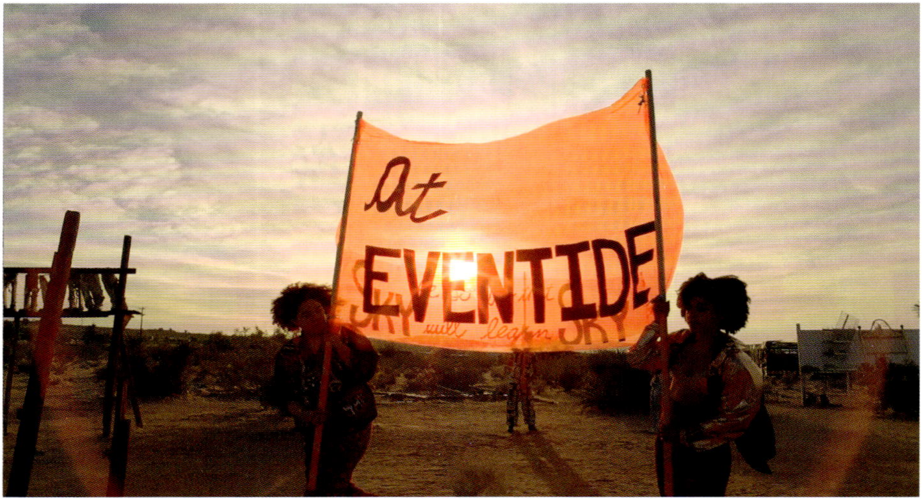

at
EVENTIDE

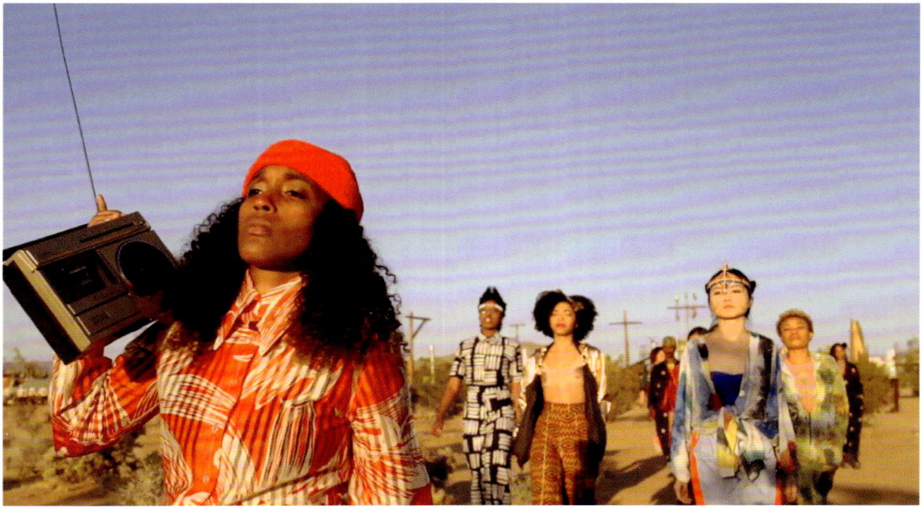

Sojourner 2018
Digital video;
colour and sound
22 min 41 sec

Is utopia achievable? What does a really radically generous community and intentional world-building look like? In *Sojourner*, filmmaker Cauleen Smith visits several different sites in the United States to observe community-building. She is searching for a utopia that we are protesting for. She believes this exists. The idea of utopia has long since been mired in cynicism, but Smith believes that there have been instances where people have managed to build intentional communities that were really successful. *Sojourner*, thus, becomes a meditation on what it means to be generous and selfless and to imagine what happens when cities put community at the centre. Protest is a fight for the future; Smith speculates what that future could look like and shines lights on examples such as the Watts Tower Community or the Shaker Community, the first and only in a city centre, started by Rebecca Cox Jackson. The film is overlaid by moving audio works: women reading texts by American jazz musician Alice Coltrane can be heard alongside contemporary texts written by the Black women, academics and queer women that make up the Combahee River Collective, serving as a manifesto and declaration for togetherness to enable liberation. The text lists the different ways Black women have been marginalised and dismissed, positing that we must save ourselves, together: 'Before looking at the recent development of Black feminism, we would like to affirm that we find our origins in the historical reality of African-American women's continuous life and their struggle for survival and liberation.' The film ends with the powerful, Black female protagonists walking through the desert, before settling into a pose and staring straight down the lens and inhaling. It's a collective reminder to just breathe, and take the daily fight of existence one day at a time.

Cauleen Smith
b.1967

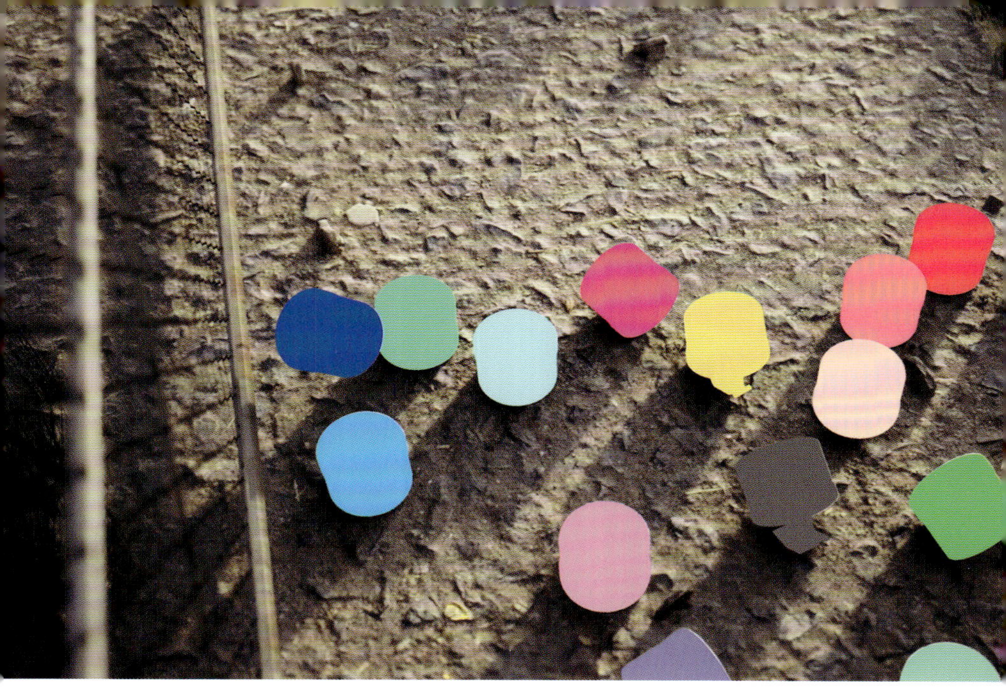

Still from
Triple-Chaser
2019. Coloured
'masks' tell the
classifier where
in the image the
Triple-Chaser
grenade exists.

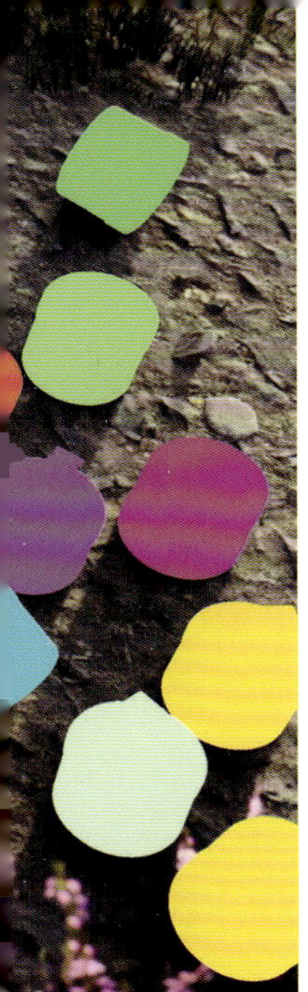

In November 2018 US Border Patrol agents fired tear gas grenades at a march of migrants and refugees gathering near the border with Mexico. Photographs showed that many of those grenades were made by the Safariland Group, one of the world's leading manufacturers of 'less lethal' munitions. The CEO of Safariland is Warren B. Kanders, who was also the vice-chair of the Board of Trustees of the Whitney Museum of Art, New York, until he was ousted in 2020, after many months of protest against his association with the group.

When Forensic Architecture, a multidisciplinary research group based at Goldsmiths, University of London, were invited to exhibit at the 2019 Whitney Biennial (which has a long tradition of dissent and protest), they responded to the controversy of Kanders's affiliation with Safariland, in a project that trained algorithmic 'computer vision' classifiers to detect the company's tear gas canisters among millions of images shared online.

Records detailing the export of military equipment from the US is public record, but tear gas and its export is not. Therefore, tracing images of tear gas canisters online is one of the only means available for monitoring organisations and the public to track where they are being exported to and for what use. In automating what is otherwise a time-consuming manual research procedure, Forensic Architecture sought to empower civil society, rally for greater transparency, advocate for the discontinuation of tear gas use as a security measure, and pursue corporate accountability in the global arms trade. An affecting film detailing how the technology works, produced in partnership with Laura Poitras's Praxis Films, was one of the star pieces in the Whitney Biennial. Museums face increasing scrutiny for upholding moral values; although the Whitney did not ask for nor participate in the development of this film, in exhibiting *Triple-Chaser* the institution faced this head-on.

Forensic Architecture
formed 2010

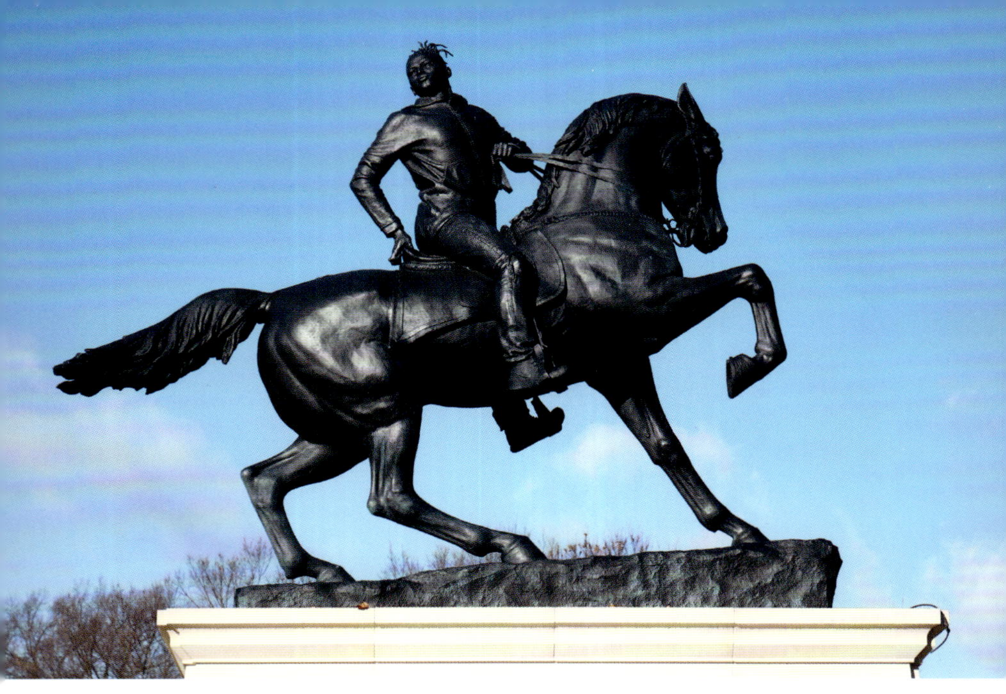

Kehinde Wiley's highly naturalistic paintings of Black figures (which include his renowned portrait of former president Barack Obama) seek to rewrite art history. Set against densely patterned backgrounds, they offer a rubric through which to engage with the fraught histories and traditions that Black people have faced. But Wiley's *Rumors of War*, a monumental bronze erected in New York's Times Square, pushes the narrative of reclaiming public space even further. Wiley presents an African American man proudly dressed in urban streetwear astride a gallant horse; his hero favours tracksuits over the britches and capes of Confederate statues. The sculpture is a powerful repositioning of young Black men, so often hit by negative stereotypes, in public consciousness. It ignited national debate surrounding monuments and their role in the telling of incomplete narratives and perpetuating contemporary inequities – before the fall of Confederate statues in 2020 – and who gets commemorated in public space. This valiant work demands more from representation and seeks to challenge deeply engrained beliefs. Public sculpture such as this highlights that diverse contemporary heroes are scarcely shown. How might society shift its preconceptions if it saw a statue of a Black man – not in the narrative of oppression, but of celebration – every day? I wonder.

Kehinde Wiley
b.1977

The Anti-Imperial Poetry of Edgar Heap of Birds maps the recursive habits of empire, and calls for a better understanding of – and relationship to – community and land. For more than forty years, Edgar Heap of Birds, an Oklahoma-based artist and academic from the Cheyenne and Arapaho nations, has, through many mediums and disciplines, been standing up and advocating for indigenous communities and rallying for social justice.

Living on tribal land since 1981, Heap of Birds has worked consistently to confront unacknowledged histories of state and settler violence against Native communities in the United States. His work is both revelatory and ruminative, as he convincingly draws parallels between historical violence and ongoing injustices to establish a legacy that gives potency to his protest. Look how little has changed, he seeks for us to understand. The world goes by, the context differs, but people are the same. His unique blend of activism and art began with his 1990 project, *Building Minnesota*, which honoured the forty men from Dakota who were killed in the largest mass execution in American history. His work wholeheartedly articulates a political position that supports land defenders, and is vehemently against militarism and capitalism.

It is all too obvious to say that history is written by the victorious, but other histories are also always being composed, and there are innumerable forms this writing can take. This is further explored in Surviving Active Shooter Custer, shown at MoMA PS1 in 2019, which highlighted the racial violence in contemporary society in America, as well as expanding this legacy to Native American life and history. Heap of Birds seeks to point a finger at the violence so deeply entrenched in global historical pasts, and how dominant cultures play a hand in the erasure of these histories and effectively 'Tipp-ex' oppression. The use of the term 'active shooter' serves to characterise and bring new life to past atrocities with contemporary language. Heap of Birds has often employed his clever use of language to condemn governmental structures, with powerful verbal juxtapositions and iconic yet idiosyncratic lyrical phrases.

Places of Healing, a forty-eight-piece monoprint installation, chronicles thirty different Native ceremonial sites across North America and Hawaii for communal healing and prayer. These sites are more than just places of acknowledgement or idols; to these communities, they are functioning places of healing, warranting visits when ill, grieving, sad, or needing to connect and reset. The installation is made up of twenty-four sheets and twenty-four corresponding 'ghost prints' – a faint second pull of the print that represents the artist's view that Native Americans are ghosts of America – and its poignancy is in the text. As with much of Heap of Birds's work, text gets into the psyche quickly. Even when it is in a language unfamiliar, perhaps more so, the viewer looks with curiosity. Text is powerful symbolism; of this, Heap of Birds is certainly aware.

Heap of Birds encourages us to consider the forces that control the world, and how much we know about the world itself. His work is a protest against the status quo and controlled knowledge. He wants us to consider the alternatives, delve deep into other histories, and challenge what we are told. His protest is the everyday eschewing of categorisation and man-made structures; in so doing, he makes his art a place of healing itself.

Edgar Heap of Birds
b.1954

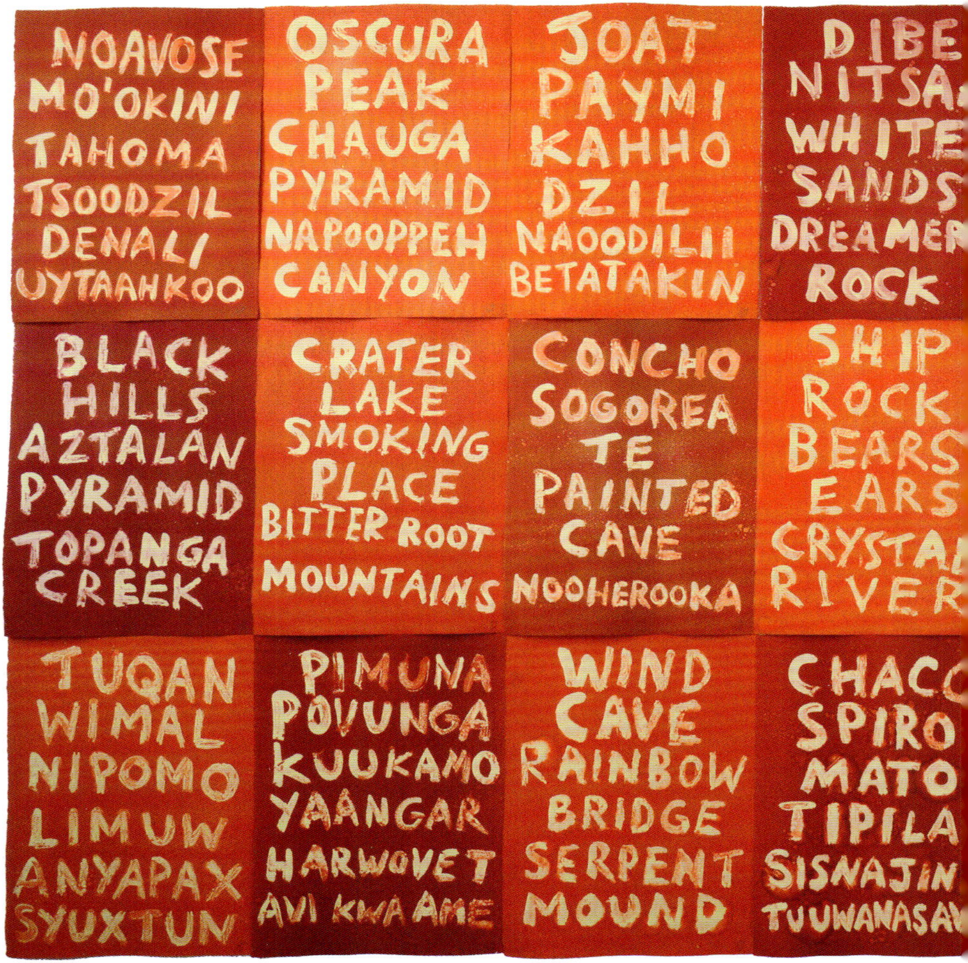

NOAVOSE
MO'OKINI
TAHOMA
TSOODZIL
DENALI
UYTAAHKOO

OSCURA
PEAK
CHAUGA
PYRAMID
NAPOOPPEH
CANYON

JOAT
PAYMI
KAHHO
DZIL
NAOODILII
BETATAKIN

DIBE
NITSA
WHITE
SANDS
DREAMER
ROCK

BLACK
HILLS
AZTALAN
PYRAMID
TOPANGA
CREEK

CRATER
LAKE
SMOKING
PLACE
BITTER ROOT
MOUNTAINS

CONCHO
SOGOREA
TE
PAINTED
CAVE
NOOHEROOKA

SHIP
ROCK
BEARS
EARS
CRYSTAL
RIVER

TUQAN
WIMAL
NIPOMO
LIMUW
ANYAPAX
SYUXTUN

PIMUNA
POVUNGA
KUUKAMO
YAANGAR
HARWOVET
AVI KWA AME

WIND
CAVE
RAINBOW
BRIDGE
SERPENT
MOUND

CHACO
SPIRO
MATO
TIPILA
SISNAJIN
TUUWANASAV

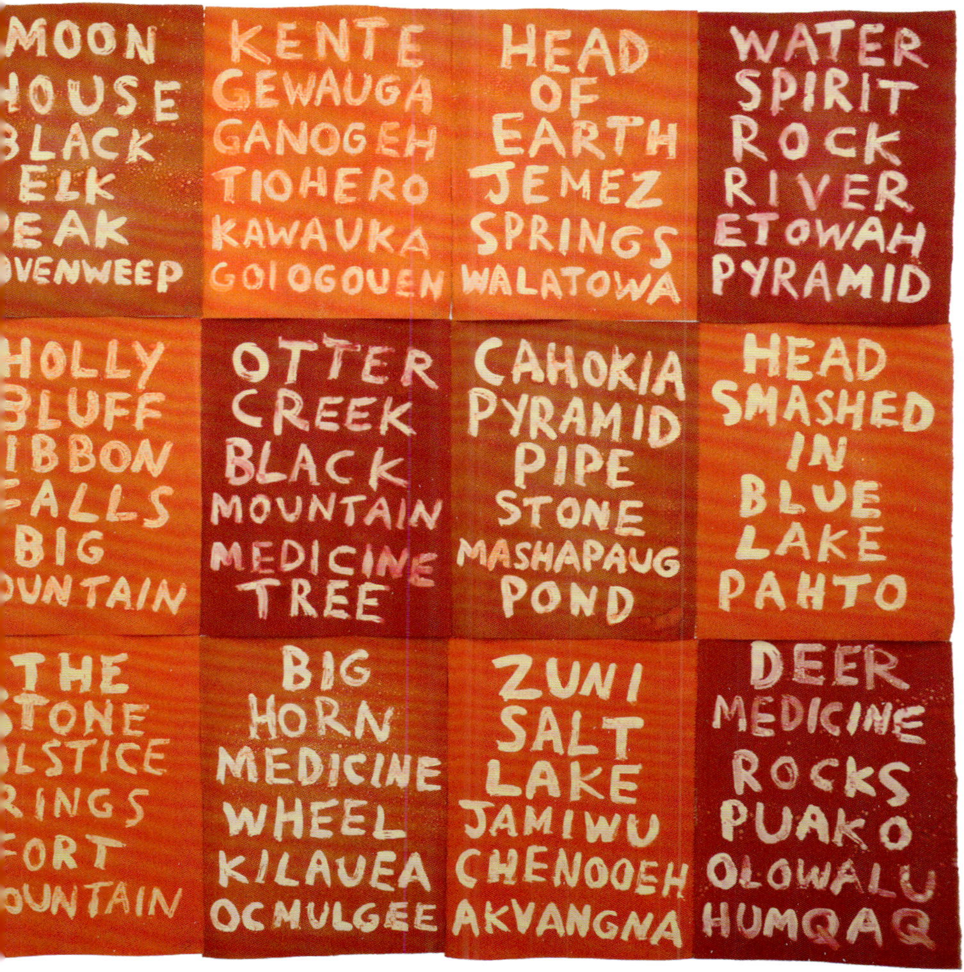

MOON
HOUSE
BLACK
ELK
PEAK
OVENWEEP

KENTE
GEWAUGA
GANOGEH
TIOHERO
KAWAUKA
GOIOGOUEN

HEAD
OF
EARTH
JEMEZ
SPRINGS
WALATOWA

WATER
SPIRIT
ROCK
RIVER
ETOWAH
PYRAMID

HOLLY
BLUFF
IBBON
ALLS
BIG
OUNTAIN

OTTER
CREEK
BLACK
MOUNTAIN
MEDICINE
TREE

CAHOKIA
PYRAMID
PIPE
STONE
MASHAPAUG
POND

HEAD
SMASHED
IN
BLUE
LAKE
PAHTO

THE
STONE
OLSTICE
RINGS
ORT
OUNTAIN

BIG
HORN
MEDICINE
WHEEL
KILAUEA
OCMULGEE

ZUNI
SALT
LAKE
JAMIWU
CHENOOEH
AKVANGNA

DEER
MEDICINE
ROCKS
PUAKO
OLOWALU
HUMQAQ

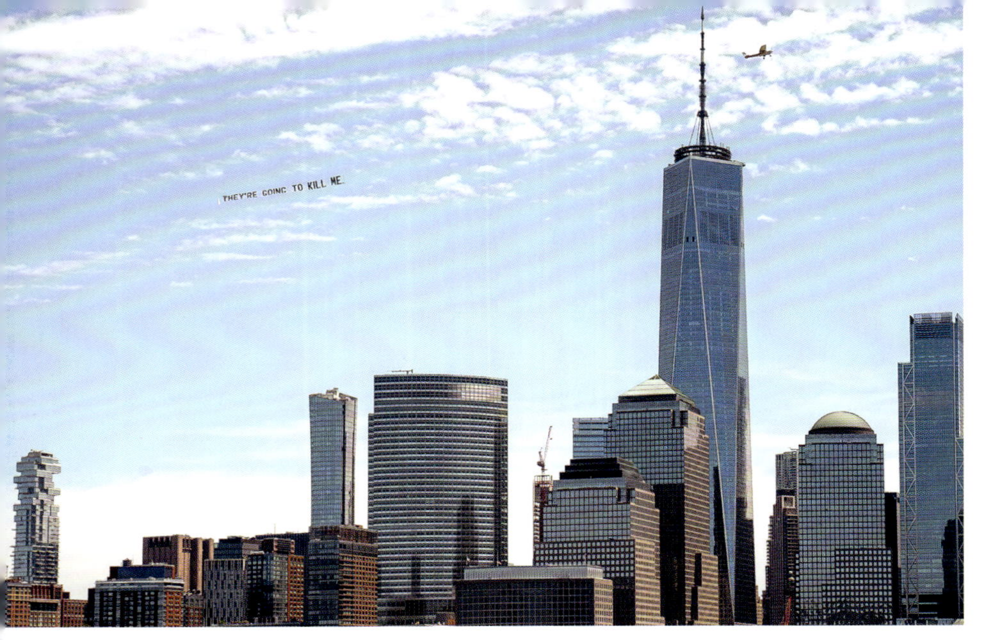
THEY'RE GOING TO KILL ME.

THEY'RE GOING TO KILL ME.

Protests can be found not only on the streets but in the skies. After the death of George Floyd in 2020, Dallas-based artist Jammie Holmes commissioned planes to fly over five US cities – New York, Miami, Dallas, Detroit and Los Angeles – with banners emblazoned with Floyd's last words, including 'They're going to kill me' and 'Please, I can't breathe'. Indeed, it took the reverberation of 'I can't breathe' worldwide for us to realise that for so long, so many have been holding their breath. Employing the simplicity of text in non-traditional media has echoes of Jenny Holzer (p.110) and Barbara Kruger (p.84), but with an added punch in the gut.

Holmes deliberately sought out the skies as an alternative to the noise of digital media to present his work. For days, videos, screenshots and photos relating to Floyd's death took over social media platforms, and it became an inescapable truth that had ripple effects around the world. Usually reserved for sporting events, gaudy marriage proposals or for advertising products or services, Holmes reclaimed a frivolous mode of information-sharing by injecting it with political intent. He refuses to let us forget the stark truth of police brutality in America when we put down our newspaper, turn off the television or close Instagram. Looking to the sky is usually a hopeful activity; disrupting this space is a forceful reminder of uncomfortable realities served with a side of aspiration.

Jammie Holmes
b.1984

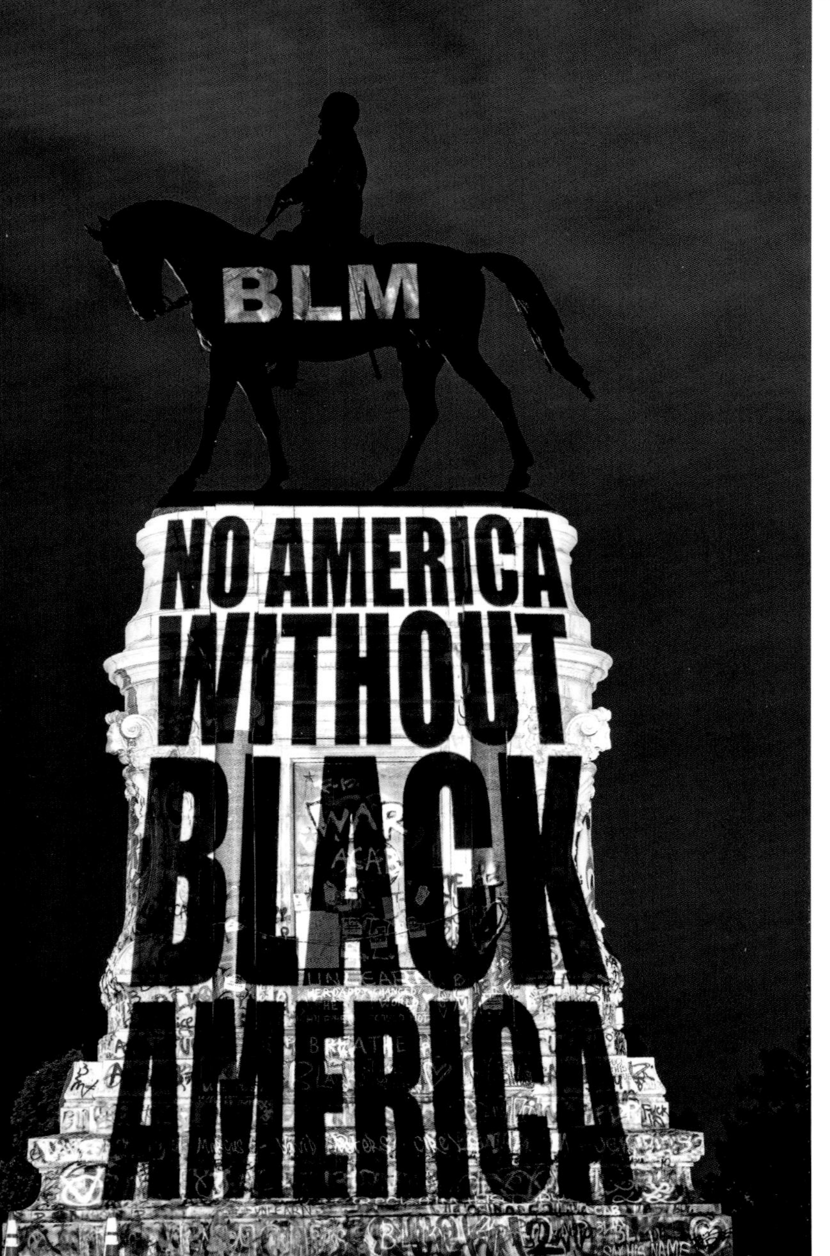

BLM
NO AMERICA
WITHOUT
BLACK
AMERICA

The ushering in of a revitalised Black Lives Matter movement, following the tragic death of George Floyd in 2020, caused ripples throughout the art world and fast-forwarded discussions pertaining to how monuments can have a living value and how to reckon with contentious public statues. In Virginia, the Robert E. Lee Monument is the only remaining Confederate statue on Richmond's historic Monument Avenue. Amid discussions of the controversial statue's removal, artist Dustin Klein employed light to alter its meaning. In the summer of 2020, Klein and the writer and artist Alex Criqui projected onto the statue images and videos of Black figures who have shaped history – Frederick Douglass, Harriet Tubman, Billie Holliday – as well as Black citizens, such as George Floyd and Breonna Taylor, whose deaths were caused by police brutality. The juxtaposition of those who have faced cruelty at the hands of police with Robert E. Lee, a slave owner, is a powerful protest for change as well as a transformation of the site into a place of healing and remembrance. And the presence of influential Black figures forces us to question who gets remembered and commemorated, and how narrow the catchment really is for those who are immortalised. Temporary and cyclical, *Reclaiming the Monument* proves that art doesn't have to last to have a lasting impact. Its immediacy is unstifled by the often time-intensive bureaucracies of the commissioning process, and it impacted millions, beyond Virginia, as images of the work ricocheted throughout the world via media and social media reportage. *Reclaiming the Monument* will continue to make us question how we perceive public statues and the legacy of cruelty against Black people, and calls for greater representation in the public realm.

Dustin Klein & Alex Criqui
b.1949

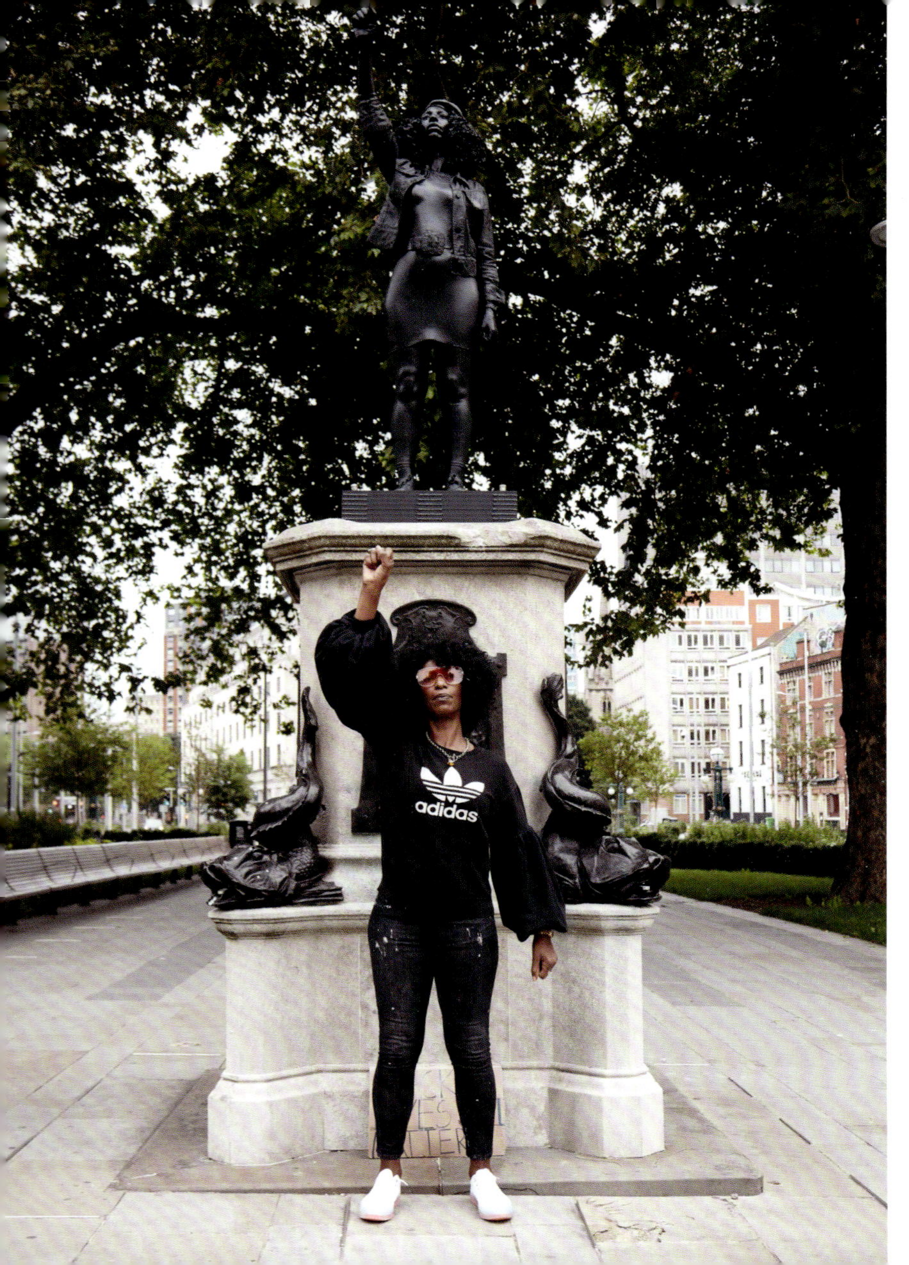

adidas

How many times have you seen a statue of a Black woman? *A Surge of Power* is a powerful testimony to the agency of Black women and their resistance and resilience. The year 2020, when the work was made, was one of reckoning. In the wake of the killing of George Floyd, conversation and debate turned to the commemoration of slave traders in our public realm. On 7 June 2020, the statue of Edward Colston, a prominent seventeenth- and eighteenth-century Bristol merchant, philanthropist and slave trader, was toppled during a George Floyd protest in Bristol, in the UK. Notably, the existence of the statue had been objected to for many years – protestors took this daily affront into their own hands and gave the statue a watery grave. After it had fallen Jen Reid, a local resident, climbed onto the plinth and made a raised fist – a Black Power salute. It is this defiant pose that inspired Quinn (after seeing a photograph of her in action) to track Reid down and collaborate on the statue. Together they erected the resin sculpture on the empty plinth under the cover of night, leaving Bristol and indeed, the rest of the world, to wake up to an almighty statement. *A Surge of Power*, which was eventually taken down by Bristol Council, encouraged debate about the visibility of Black people in public art, as well as allyship, authorship and reprising the idea that such art should interrogate the issues of the time. It was a wrecking ball in the face of complacency – and sent ripples through the art world. Isn't that what art is supposed to do anyway?

Marc Quinn & Jen Reid
b.1964 & 1970

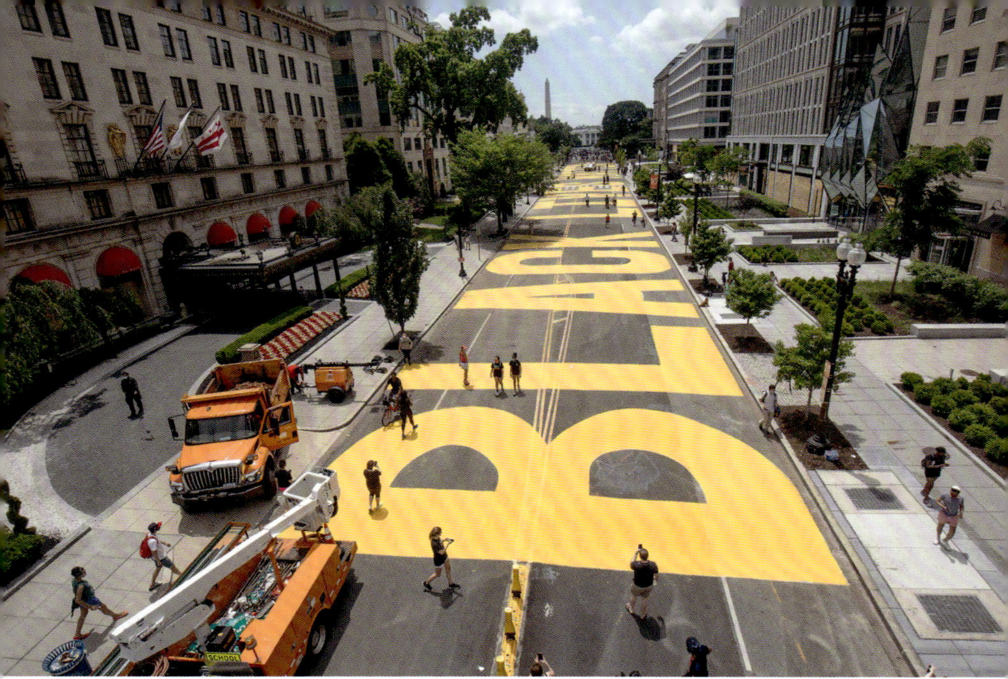

Despite a global pandemic, 2020 was the year of protest and marked a resurgence of the Black Lives Matter movement. After the death of George Floyd, murals began to emerge documenting people's reactions to this tumultuous moment. On 5 June 2020, during the George Floyd protests, the DC Public Works Department of Washington, assisted by the Murals DC programme, painted the words BLACK LIVES MATTER in eleven-metre-tall yellow capital letters, stretching two blocks, on 16th Street Northwest. Triumphantly civic, this bold championing of racial equality, painted in road paint used for street centrelines, is accompanied by the DC flag. The location is poignant: directly in front of Lafayette Square (which protestors had been occupying), just outside of the White House – a blatant anti-Trump symbol, with its canary-yellow battle-cry becoming a runway to the white gates, as if to point to the problem. On the same day, the District of Columbia Mayor Muriel Bowser announced that part of the street had been officially renamed Black Lives Matter Plaza. The bright yellow letters are a daily reminder to the citizens of DC to heed their message. The message is poetically simple, and a shining example of how public art can impact society. It is a permanent protest placard, its potent political message crying out underfoot as pedestrians and drivers pass by.

Various artists

James Attlee, *Guernica: Painting the End of the World (The Landmark Library)*, London 2017.

Carol Becker, Achim Borchardt-Hume and Lisa Lee, *Theaster Gates (Phaidon Contemporary Artists Series)*, London 2015.

Anthony Downey, *Art and Politics Now*, London and New York 2014.

Mark Godfrey and Allie Biswas, *The Soul of a Nation Reader: Writings by and about Black American Artists, 1960-1980*, New York 2021.

Daniel Herwitz, *The Political Power of Visual Art: Liberty, Solidarity, and Rights*, London and New York 2021.

bell hooks, *Art on My Mind: Visual Politics*, New York 1995.

Robert Klanten, M. Hubner and A. Bieber, *Art & Agenda: Political Art and Activism*, Berlin and London 2011.

Christian Viveros-Fauné, *Social Forms: A Short History of Political Art*, New York 2018.

Credits

Library Street Collective p.149
The Jacob and Gwendolyn Lawrence
Foundation/ Art Resource, NY pp.2, 30
Courtesy the Prints & Photographs
Division, Library of Congress,
Washington, D.C   p.62

© MRBAB/ photo: J. Geleyns p.10
Peter Macdiarmid/ Getty Images p.86
Attilio Maranzano p.110
© 2022 The Museum of Modern Art, New
York/ Scala, Florence pp.38–9, 54,
88, 90, 94–5, 102
The Phillips Collection, Washington,
D.C. p.26
Pitkin Studio/ Art Resource, NY p.98
© Courtesy the Pushkin State Museum
of Fine Arts, Moscow pp.28–9
Photographic Archives Museo Nacional
Centro de Reina Sofia, Madrid
pp.24–5

Artwork approved by the Norman
Rockwell Family Agency p.32
Bob Sabin p.42
Robert Abbott Sengstacke/ Getty
Images pp.40–1
Courtesy Smoking Dogs Films and
Lisson Gallery p.78
Parisa Taghizadeh, courtesy the
artist p.106 (top)
© Tate front cover, pp.15, 19, 36,
50, 60, 66, 68, 70, 72, 80, 104, 106
(bottom), 112, 118–19

© Victoria and Albert Museum p.44

© Ai Weiwei Studio. Courtesy Ai
Weiwei Studio pp.100, 114–15
Ted West, courtesy the artist
pp.146–7
© 2022 Whitney Museum of American
Art/ Licensed by Scala pp.52, 58,
82–3, 92

Copyright credits:

All works are © the artist(s) unless
otherwise stated here below.
© The Ardeshir Trust p.62
Tania Bruguera © ARS, NY and DACS,
London 2022 p.102
© Catlett Mora Family Trust/ VAGA at
ARS, NY and DACS, London 2022 p.48
© Agnes Denes, courtesy Leslie
Tonkonow Artworks + Projects,
New York p.74
© Emory Douglas/ DACS 2022 p.44

© Forensic Architecture/ Praxis
Films pp.140–1
© courtesy www.guerrillagirls.com
p.80
© Felix Gonzalez-Torres, courtesy
the Felix Gonzalez-Torres Foundation
p.90
© Estate of Philip Guston, courtesy
Hauser & Wirth p.46
© Estate of Richard Hamilton p.72
© Keith Haring Foundation pp.82–3
© Jenny Holzer. ARS, NY and DACS,
London 2022 pp.15, 110
© Estate of Nancy Reddin Kienholz.
Courtesy L.A. Louver p.52
© The Jacob and Gwendolyn Knight
Lawrence Foundation, Seattle/
Artists Rights Society (ARS), New
York and DACS, London 2022 pp.2,
26, 30
© Glenn Ligon; courtesy Thomas Dane
Gallery, London p.104
© Estate of Donald Locke p.19
Joe Minter © ARS, NY and DACS,
London 2022 p.98
© Succession Picasso/ DACS, London
2022 pp.24–5
© Faith Ringgold/ ARS, NY and DACS,
London, courtesy ACA Galleries, New
York 2022 pp.38–9, 54

© Banco de México Diego Rivera Frida
Kahlo Museums Trust, Mexico, D.F./
DACS 2022 pp.28–9
© Chéri Samba, courtesy Galerie
MAGNIN-A, Paris p.108
© Smoking Dogs Films, All Rights
Reserved, DACS 2022 p.78
© The Nancy Spero and Leon Golub
Foundation for the Arts/VAGA at ARS,
NY and DACS, London 2022 p.76

Courtesy the estate of May Stevens
and RYAN LEE Gallery, New York p.58
© Kara Walker, courtesy Sikkema
Jenkins & Co., New York; Sprüth
Magers, Berlin pp.94–5

© 2022 The Andy Warhol Foundation
for the Visual Arts, Inc./ Licensed
by DACS, London p.36

© Ai Weiwei Studio pp.100, 114–15

© Kehinde Wiley. Presented by Times
Square Arts in partnership with the
Virginia Museum of Fine Art and Sean
Kelly, New York p.142